INDEPENDENT STUDY PROGRAM

Susan K. Johnsen
Baylor University

Kay Johnson
Educational Consultant

ISBN 1-882664-16-7

P.O. Box 8813 ▼ Waco ▼ TX ▼ 76714 ▼ (817) 756-3337 ▼ FAX (817) 756-3339

to our families...

    David, Paul, Molly, Becky, James

to our colleagues who supported this independent study product...

    Terry Masters, Gail Tucker-Mills, Shirley Henderson, Nancy Arulf, Sue Clover, Dorothy Stroud,

    the teachers and students who "tried it out"

and for inspiration...

    Sandra Kaplan and Don Treffinger

TABLE OF CONTENTS

Overview   viii

Independent Study Program Lessons

Introduction

      Lesson 1:   Introduction to Independent Study   1

Select a Topic

      Lesson 2:   Topic Selection   4
      Lesson 3:   Topic Selection: Gathering Information   7

Organize a Topic

      Lesson 4:   Topic Organization: Introduction; Descriptions   9
      Lesson 5:   Topic Organization: Comparisons   11
      Lesson 6:   Topic Organization: Causes and Effects   13
      Lesson 7:   Topic Organization: Problems and Solutions   15

Ask Questions

      Lesson 8:   Ask "W" Questions   17
      Lesson 9:   Ask Higher Level Thinking Questions   19
      Lesson 10: Identify and Sequence Questions for Study   24

Use à Study Method

      Lesson 11: Introduction to Study Method   26
      Lesson 12: Nonbiased Samples   35
      Lesson 13: Development of Objective Measures   38
      Lesson 14: Data Analysis and Summary   40

Collect Information

      Lesson 15: Collect Information   46
      Lesson 16: Collect Information: Brainstorm   48
      Lesson 17: Collect Information: Classify   51
      Lesson 18: Collect Information: Interview   53
      Lesson 19: Collect Information: Summarize   57
      Lesson 20: Collect Information: Survey   60
      Lesson 21: Collect Information: Note Taking   64
      Lesson 22: Collect Information: Note Taking--Outlining   68
      Lesson 23: Collect Information: Write Letters   73

Develop a Product

      Lesson 24: Overview   77

Present the Product

      Lesson 25: Overview   91

Evaluate the Study

Lesson 26: Evaluation   94

Appendix A: Selected References   98

Appendix B: Resources   100

Overhead Masters   102
Handouts   114
Skill Sequence   118
Correlation Chart   120
Record Forms   126

Index   130

THERE IS ALWAYS·
ONE MOMENT IN
CHILDHOOD WHEN
·THE DOOR
OPENS·
AND LETS THE
FUTURE IN ·:·
GRAHAM GREEN·

It must be remembered that the purpose of education is not to fill the minds of students with facts;
it is not to reform them, or amuse them, or to make them expert technicians in any field.
It is to teach them to think, if that is possible, and always to think for themselves.

Robert Hutchins

PROGRAM OVERVIEW

Independent study involves the in-depth learning of topics that are of interest to the student. While students are often eager to pursue these interesting areas of study, they lack the skills necessary in achieving their goals. While many fine independent study materials are available to the classroom teacher, we found that few provided the framework needed for teaching the entire independent study process.

This program has been under development for five years and has been classroom tested with thousands of students at all grade levels. It attempts to provide the framework necessary for independent learning. Consequently, the content (*i.e.*, the topic to be studied) is left to you, the teacher, or to your students.

PROGRAM COMPONENTS

Teacher's Guide

The Teacher's Guide provides a detailed listing of skill sequences, correlations, classroom management ideas and alternate procedures for teaching each lesson. It contains step-by-step lessons related to the eight steps of basic research: select a topic, organize a topic, ask questions, use a study method, collect information, develop a product, present information, evaluate the study.

Resource Cards

The Resource Cards cover all of the steps of basic research and are correlated to each lesson in the Teacher's Guide. These reusable cards may be used by the students independently and/or as teaching materials for each lesson.

Student Booklets

The Student Booklet is a write-in workbook which is correlated to the Teacher's Guide and is used for instruction and to help organize the student's independent study. This booklet is adapted for both elementary and secondary students.

SKILL SEQUENCE

Specific skills are listed for each of the areas of basic research (see Independent Study Skill Sequence, Appendix B, page 118). These skills are clustered and arranged linearly from selecting a topic to evaluation. This arrangement, however, does not preclude the knowledgeable teacher's rearrangement. In fact, this rearrangement is encouraged in adapting instruction to individual differences and enhancing the circular process of independent study. For example, the authors have found that some teachers teach "note taking" and "outlining" before beginning the program; others omit the *Organize a Topic* and *Use a Study Method* sections, teaching only "descriptions" and "collecting factual information," until the students have mastered skills in the other sections; and others teach only one or two of the skills in each area, increasing the number as the students become more proficient. The teacher will be able to locate and select program materials for specific skills in the Correlation Chart (see Appendix B, pages 120-125).

USING THE INDEPENDENT STUDY PROGRAM

Procedure:

1. Read the Independent Study Skill Sequence (see Appendix B, page 118).

2. Identify which skills will be taught to your class during the first independent study. (As you teach, you may modify this skill list as you discover the students' levels.)

NOTE: Remember to select a small number of skills for the first study. You will want the students to complete their first study in a short period of time (*i.e.*, less than three weeks) so that they are able to experience the entire process successfully! An example first study:

The teacher selects a topic for the students to study. Together they ask some "W" questions and collect information through interviews. The products are diagrams, graphs, and tape recordings. These products are set up in a display during the school open house with students as on-going presenters. The study is evaluated by the teacher, individual students and the audience at the open house.

3. On the group record form, list the students' names who will be participating in the independent study (see Appendix B, page 126). Write the first area that you will be covering at the top of this form. List the skills in the boxes at the top.

   (As each student completes a skill, write the date beside the student's name under the skill completed.)

INDEPENDENT STUDY SKILL SEQUENCE

INTRODUCTION

1. Can name and describe the steps of independent study
2. Can tell what a topic is

SELECT A TOPIC

1. Can brainstorm topics
2. Can gather information about topic
3. Can select one topic using an evaluation procedure
   a. Can identify criteria for selecting a topic
   b. Can rate topics according to criteria

ORGANIZE A TOPIC

1. Can organize a topic using descriptions
   a. Can brainstorm characteristics
   b. Can use a network in describing a topic
2. Can organize a topic using comparisons
   a. Can brainstorm comparisons
   b. Can use a chart in comparing topics
3. Can organize a topic using causes and effects
   a. Can brainstorm changes, causes, and/or effects
   b. Can use a chart in examining changes, causes, effects
4. Can organize a topic using problems and solutions
   a. Can brainstorm problems and/or solutions
   b. Can use SCAMPER techniques for problems, solutions

ASK QUESTIONS

1. Can identify good study questions
2. Can write good study questions using "W" words
3. Can write questions requiring little thinking
4. Can write questions requiring more thinking
5. Can write questions requiring most thinking
6. Can select questions using an evaluation procedure
   a. Can identify criteria for selecting questions
   b. Can rate questions according to criteria
7. Can organize questions into a sequence for study
   a. Can develop a sequence with questions
   b. Can place these questions into outline form

USE A STUDY METHOD

1. Can describe topic with numbers or facts
2. Can examine past or history of a topic
3. Can look at development of topic
4. Can observe a person, a group or something closely
5. Can compare one thing with another using numbers
6. Can examine an improvement made to a problem
7. Can conduct experimental research
8. Can collect factual information
9. Can select a nonbiased sample
10. Can examine reliability of research instrument
11. Can examine validity of research instrument
12. Can make valid generalizations about study
13. Can describe topic using the average, mode and range
14. Can examine relationships using correlations

© Johnson and Johnson, 1986   118

COLLECT INFORMATION

1. Can brainstorm
   a. Can use SCAMPER skills
   b. Can evaluate brainstorm list
2. Can classify
3. Can interview
4. Can summarize
   a. Can make generalizations
   b. Can describe the parts
   c. Can identify causes and effects
   d. Can make comparisons
   e. Can show a sequence
   f. Can identify problems and solutions
5. Can conduct a survey
   a. Can conduct a face-to-face interview
   b. Can conduct a telephone interview
   c. Can develop a questionnaire
   d. Can analyze results
6. Can take notes
7. Can outline
   a. Can outline main ideas
   b. Can outline subtopics
   c. Can outline details
8. Can write a business letter

DEVELOP A PRODUCT

1. Can brainstorm products
2. Can select a product
   a. Can identify criteria for selecting a product
   b. Can rate products according to criteria
3. Can plan the development of product
4. Can develop a product
   a. Book
   b. Diagram
   c. Diorama
   d. Filmstrip
   e. Game
   f. Graph
   g. Poster
   h. Puppet Show
   i. Report
   j. Tape Recording
   k. Television Show
   l. Time line
   m. Other_____

PRESENT THE PRODUCT

1. Can present the product orally
2. Can use a display
3. Other_____

EVALUATE THE STUDY

1. Can do a self evaluation
2. Can compare own evaluation

INDEPENDENT STUDY AREA _____

SKILL

STUDENT NAME															

126

USING THE INDEPENDENT STUDY PROGRAM

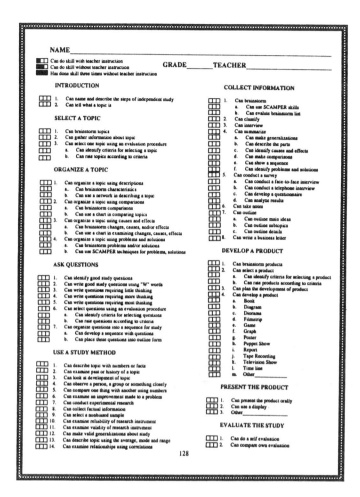

Procedure:

4. You may also want to use the individual record form to keep track of progress as your independent study program becomes more individualized and as a record for subsequent grades (see Appendix B, page 128). On separate forms fill in the names of individual students who will be participating in the Independent Study Program.

   [This form may be used for three levels of mastery: acquisition, maintenance and proficiency. When the student is able to demonstrate the skill for the **first time with teacher instruction**, the first box is filled (*i.e.*, acquisition). When the student has demonstrated the skill the second time, **without direct teacher instruction**, the second box is filled (*i.e.*, maintenance). When the student has demonstrated the skill at least **three times without teacher instruction** the third box is filled (*i.e.*, proficiency). In this way, varying degrees of skill mastery can be indicated.]

5. Put your record forms in a notebook for easy reference and recording.

6. If you are going to allow the students to use the Resource Cards as an independent learning activity, place these cards along with other related resources in an area of your room.

7. If you are going to use other resources, add these to the correlation chart for future reference (see Appendix B for other materials on Independent Study).

8. Look at the teacher lessons. Get the materials that you will need from the Teacher's Guide, Student Booklet and Resource Cards for the first lesson that you will be teaching.

9. Begin and have fun learning!

There is danger in probing the future with too short a stick. Excellence takes time.
-E. Dale

S.K.J. and K.J.

the best and most important
part of every person's education
is that which they give themselves.
e. gibbon

INDEPENDENT STUDY PROGRAM LESSONS

LESSON 1. INTRODUCTION TO INDEPENDENT STUDY

Concepts: 1. Independent Study
                  2. Topic

Objective: Given an independent study plan, the students will describe the steps in independent study.

Materials: 1. Student Booklet, pages 1, 2, 3, 4
                  2. Resource Cards 1, 2, 3
                  3. Blank overhead or chalk/chalkboard

Evaluation: Given an independent study plan, are students able to describe each step?

(**Note for Group Independent Study:** If you would like the students to work together as a group, follow each step as if the group is going to work on a single topic area. However, students may choose to study different aspects of the same topic.)

Procedure:

1. Write on the overhead or chalkboard the words "Independent Study." Ask the students for examples of what they think these words mean.

2. Write their responses on the overhead or chalkboard.

3. Write the definition for independent study using their examples or the one listed in the **Student Booklet, page 1.**

4. Distribute the Student Booklets. Have the students write their names on the front of their booklets.

5. Have students open the **Student Booklet** to **page 1.**

6. Tell what they will do during each step.

7. Have the students check the steps that they will do during their first independent study.

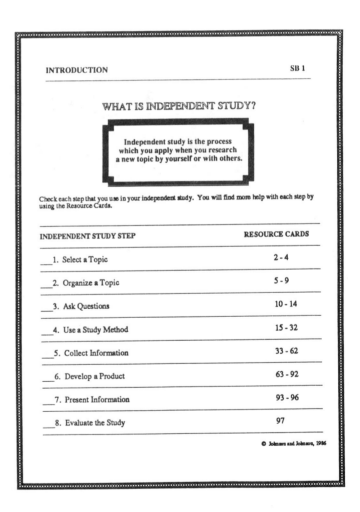

INTRODUCTION   SB 1

WHAT IS INDEPENDENT STUDY?

Independent study is the process which you apply when you research a new topic by yourself or with others.

Check each step that you use in your independent study. You will find more help with each step by using the Resource Cards.

INDEPENDENT STUDY STEP	RESOURCE CARDS
___ 1. Select a Topic	2 - 4
___ 2. Organize a Topic	5 - 9
___ 3. Ask Questions	10 - 14
___ 4. Use a Study Method	15 - 32
___ 5. Collect Information	33 - 62
___ 6. Develop a Product	63 - 92
___ 7. Present Information	93 - 96
___ 8. Evaluate the Study	97

© Johnson and Johnson, 1986

INTRODUCTION SB 2

INDEPENDENT STUDY PLAN

NAME _____ DATE STARTED _____

TEACHER _____ DATE DUE _____

GENERAL INFORMATION   **DATE DUE**

1. Name of Topic _____ _____
2. Organization _____ _____
3. Specific Question _____ _____
   _____
4. Method of Study _____ _____

COLLECT INFORMATION

___ Books   ___ Field Trips   ___ Filmstrips

___ Interviews   ___ Collections   ___ Reference Books

___ Surveys   ___ Letters   ___ Observations

___ Experiments   ___ Magazines   ___ Museums

___ Movies/Films   ___ Newspapers   ___ T.V./Radio

___ Other: _____

*The end of reading
is not more books
but more life.* — H. Jackson

© Johnsen and Johnson, 1986

Procedure:

8. Have the students look at their Independent Study Plans in the **Student Booklets, pages 2 and 3**. Tell them that this plan will help them organize their independent studies.

9. If the students are going to share their products with a particular audience, tell them the type of group who will use their products or who will hear their information.

NOTE: Students will do a better job if they feel that their product(s) are really going to be used!

10. Fill in any due dates that are currently known.

NOTE: Dates are helpful in getting students to organize their time throughout the independent study.

11. If students are going to select their own topics, have a few students volunteer names of topics that they may be interested in studying and that may be interesting to the selected audience.

WHAT IS HONORED IN A COUNTRY WILL BE CULTIVATED THERE. PLATO

INTRODUCTION SB 3

DEVELOP THE PRODUCT   **DATE DUE**

1. Audience

   ___ My Class   ___ Competition

   ___ My School   ___ Other: _____

2. Product Plan

   ___ Journal   ___ Booklet   ___ T.V. Show

   ___ Model   ___ Display   ___ Written Report

   ___ Slide Show   ___ Collection   ___ Shadow Box

   ___ Poster   ___ Game   ___ Puppet Show

   ___ Graph   ___ Diagram   ___ Tape Recording

   ___ Chart   ___ Play   ___ Time Line

   ___ Other: _____

3. Final Product   _____

PRESENT THE PRODUCT   _____

EVALUATE THE STUDY

   ___ Self   ___ Teacher

   ___ Others _____

© Johnsen and Johnson, 1986

Procedure:

12. Introduce the students to the Resource Cards. Explain how the Resource Cards may be used: (1) as a review of a skill that the teacher has introduced, (2) as an introduction to a skill that they might need in their independent studies, or (3) as additional examples of skills they are using. Put **Resource Card 1** on an overhead to show the students that Resource Cards accompany each independent study step.

13. Read **Resource Cards 2 and 3** and/or have the students look at their **Student Booklets, page 4,** to show them the variety of topics that may be available to study.

14. **ASSIGNMENT**: Tell students to think about what (or what aspect of the selected topic) they would like to study and bring topics to the next meeting. They might want to review **Resource Cards 2 and 3.**

INDEX   **RESOURCE CARD**   1

INDEPENDENT STUDY STEP	CARD NUMBERS
1. Select a Topic	2 - 4
2. Organize a Topic	5 - 9
3. Ask Questions	10 - 14
4. Use a Study Method	15 - 32
5. Collect Information	33 - 62
6. Develop the Product	63 - 92
7. Present the Product	93 - 96
8. Evaluate the Study	97

SELECT A TOPIC   **RESOURCE CARD**   2

HOW DO I CHOOSE A TOPIC?

A problem I want to solve is _____.

A fact I want to prove is _____.

Something I want to learn to do is _____.

Something I want to know more about is _____.

© Johnsen & Johnson, 1986

SELECT A TOPIC   SB 4

WHAT IS A TOPIC?

A topic is the name of the subject or the main idea that you will study. Topics help you organize and classify large pieces of information into a word or phrase.

How do I choose a topic?

• A problem I want to solve is _____

_____

• A fact I want to prove is _____

_____

• Something I want to learn to do is _____

_____

• Something I want to know more about is _____

_____

• Other topics that interest me are _____

_____

© Johnsen and Johnson, 1986

SELECT A TOPIC   **RESOURCE CARD**   3

EXAMPLES OF TOPICS

A: animals, archaeology, S. B. Anthony, advertising, alphabets, astronauts, Appalachia
B: birds, book binding, braille, banks, bears, brain, banjos, bighorn sheep, Bach, Beowulf
C: computers, cars, careers, calligraphy, chess, children, climate, cultures, comics, comets
D: dance, dinosaurs, detectives, disasters, dreams, da Vinci, Disney, dolls, diseases, dolphins
E: energy, electricity, emotions, ecology, eyes, electrons, elves, eclipse, ego, English sonnets
F: fish, fashion, future, football, flutes, free will, folklore, fables, fairy tales, faults, fear, figs
G: geology, genetics, genealogy, gymnastics, Georgia, gliders, greed, games, Greenwich time
H: horses, health, heros, hospitals, hives, hematology, humor, hieroglyphs, harpsichords
I: insects, inventions, ice skating, Incas, industry, imagination, injuries, infections, intelligence
J: jazz, jellyfish, jukebox, justice, journalists, junkyards, juggling, jogging, judicial system
K: M. L. King, koala bears, Korea, kidneys, kindergarten, kiwi birds, kayaking, kaleidoscopes
L: languages, legends, laws, love, laser beams, log cabins, lady bugs, latitude, lava, learning

More examples are on the back...

LESSON 2. TOPIC SELECTION

Concepts:	1. Topic
	2. Brainstorm
	3. Evaluation

Objective: After completing a search of general topics, the student(s) will select a specific topic to study.

Materials:
1. Student Booklet, pages 2, 5, 6
2. Resource Cards 4 and 34
3. Teacher Guide, Lesson 16, pages 48-50
4. OH1 (Overhead transparency, page 102 in Teacher's Guide)
5. Blank overhead or chalkboard

Evaluation: Given five topics, can the student evaluate each and select the best one to study?

(**Note for Group Independent Study**: If you would like the students to work together as a group, follow each step as if the group is going to work on a single topic area. When you get to step 6, have the students turn to page 6 in their Student Booklets and evaluate the identified topics together.)

Procedure:

1. Tell the students that they are going to use the process of brainstorming to identify many interesting topics that they might choose to study. (See **Resource Card 34** and **Teacher Guide, Lesson 16, pages 48-50**, for more information on brainstorming.)

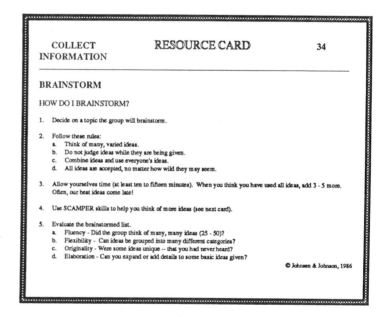

2. Write the brainstorming rules on the chalkboard or overhead:

   • Think of many, varied ideas.
   • Do not judge ideas while they are being given.
   • Combine ideas and use everyone's ideas.
   • All ideas are accepted, no matter how wild they may seem.

3. Review these rules. Give examples of "evaluating ideas."

4. Give students a minute to think of topics that they are interested in studying. With the entire group, brainstorm possible topics for 5 to 10 minutes, or until they have exhausted all of their ideas. Write all of the ideas on the board as they are given.

Procedure:

5. Use **Student Booklet, page 5** to explain how to evaluate systematically several topics in order to select the most appropriate one to study.

6. Put **OH1** on the overhead. Randomly select three to five topics from the board to judge. Write them on the lines under "Topics." (If the students are going to conduct a group study, have them vote on five topics to evaluate.)

7. Explain that in order to select the best topic the students need to think of reasons or criteria by which they might judge their topics. Ask students why they might choose to study a particular topic (see **Resource Card 4** for more examples). Give a few examples to get them started:

   Which topic is the *most* interesting to me?
   Which topic can I find the *most* information about?
   Which topic can I study *best* with the time that I have?
   Which topic can I study *best* with the resources that I have?

8. Decide on three criteria and write them on the lines at the top of the chart.

9. Look at one criterion at a time. Ask the question and then put a "5" (or the number of topics you are judging) in the box next to the topic that best fits the criterion. Put a "4" next to the topic that is the next best. Do the same with the numbers "3," "2," and "1."

10. When they have judged each question against each criterion, add the numbers next to each solution and put the sum in the "Total" box. The highest total may be the best topic to study.

SELECT A TOPIC   SB 5

HOW DO I EVALUATE THE TOPICS?

1. Select five topics to judge. Write these topics on the lines.

2. Think of some reasons (criteria) by which you will judge your topics.

3. Decide on three criteria and write them on the lines at the top of the chart by "A," "B," and "C."

4. Look at the first reason (criterion A). Ask the question and then put a "5" in the box next to the topic that best fits the criterion. Put a "4" next to the topic that is next best. Do the same with the numbers "3," "2," and "1." Next, look at the second reason (criterion B). Follow the same process. Finally, look at the third reason (criterion C).

5. Add the numbers next to each topic and put the sum in the "Total" box. The highest total may be the best topic to study. Write it on your Independent Study Plan (ISP).

EXAMPLE:

	C. Which is the most interesting topic?			
CRITERIA B. Which is the most useful topic?				T O T A L
A. Which will have information easy to find?				
TOPICS		A	B	C
1. advertising				
2. photography				
3. oceanography				
4. pollution				
5. robotics				

adapted from Texas Future Problem Solving

© Johnsen and Johnson, 1986

OH1 _____

EVALUATION CHART

	C. _____			
CRITERIA B. _____				T O T A L
A. _____				
		A	B	C
1.				
2.				
3.				
4.				
5.				

adapted from Texas Future Problem Solving

© Johnsen & Johnson, 1986

<table>
<tr><td>

SELECT A TOPIC   RESOURCE CARD   4

WHAT ARE SOME REASONS OR CRITERIA FOR CHOOSING A TOPIC?

- Which topic is the most interesting to me?
- Which topic do I know the least about?
- Which topic do I know the most about?
- Which topic will be easy to find information?
- Which topic is the most unusual?
- Which topic would be the most useful to me?

© Johnson & Johnson, 1986

</td></tr>
</table>

Procedure:

11. Have students turn to **Student Booklet, page 6** and complete the evaluation process for their selected topics of interest. Students may need help on some decisions, such as on which topic they could find the most information. Circulate around the room, assisting when needed.

NOTE: Omit this step if the students are doing a Group Independent Study.

12. Have them write their selected topic(s) on their Independent Study Plans in the **Student Booklets, page 2.**

SELECT A TOPIC   SB 6

TOPIC EVALUATION CHART

Directions: Follow the example on SB 5. Write the reasons you might study a topic beside A, B, and C. List five topics on the lines. Read Criterion A and put a "5" beside the topic that best fits that reason. Put a "4" by the next best topic, and so on to "1." Rank topics using Criteria B and C in the same way.

CRITERIA   C. _____

B. _____

A. _____   **T O T A L**

TOPICS   A   B   C

TOPICS	A	B	C	TOTAL
1.				
2.				
3.				
4.				
5.				

adapted from Texas Future Problem Solving

© Johnson and Johnson, 1986

LESSON 3. TOPIC SELECTION: GATHERING INFORMATION

Concepts:
        1. Resource
        2. Interview
        3. Card Catalogue
        4. Skimming

Objective:
        Given a list of possible resources, the student will gather general information about the topic and finalize this selection or identify a new topic.

Materials:
        1. Teacher Guide, Lesson 18, pages 53-56
        2. Resource Cards 38, 39, 40
        2. Blank overhead or chalkboard

Evaluation:
        Given a list of possible resources, can the student gather information about the topic and finalize this selection or identify a new topic?

(Note for Group Independent Study: If you would like the students to work together as a group, follow each step as a group. The final assignment might be to identify different areas within the topic that might be interesting to individuals within the group.)

Procedure:

1. Tell the group that students often change their minds about topics they identify in the beginning after they look for general information. Some reasons for the changes are these:
   - They can't find any information.
   - The information is too technical or too difficult to understand.
   - The topic is not interesting to them.
   - They find another topic that is more interesting.

2. Tell the students that it is important to find general information about their topics to decide if the topics are really the ones that they want to study.

3. Brainstorm with the students all the possible resources that could help them find general information about their proposed topics:
   - Call museums.
   - Call departments at universities.
   - Put bulletins in the teacher's lounge requesting information on topics.
   - Send home letters to parents asking for magazines, articles, resource persons or any information.
   - Look in the card catalogue in the school library; skim resources.
   - Call public radio and television stations.

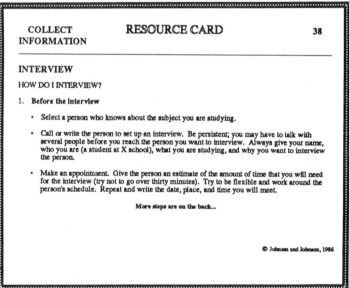

COLLECT INFORMATION   **RESOURCE CARD**   **38**

INTERVIEW

HOW DO I INTERVIEW?

1. **Before the interview**
   - Select a person who knows about the subject you are studying.
   - Call or write the person to set up an interview. Be persistent; you may have to talk with several people before you reach the person you want to interview. Always give your name, who you are (a student at X school), what you are studying, and why you want to interview the person.
   - Make an appointment. Give the person an estimate of the amount of time that you will need for the interview (try not to go over thirty minutes). Try to be flexible and work around the person's schedule. Repeat and write the date, place, and time you will meet.

More steps are on the back...

© Johnsen and Johnson, 1986

38b

INTERVIEW

STEPS (continued):
   - Do your homework; know who the person is, why he/she might be helpful to you, and learn something about the interviewee before the interview.
   - Make some notes to take into the interview: name of person being interviewed, date and time of interview, position or occupation of person, why this person was selected, the topic that will be discussed, background information on the person.
   - Write a list of questions you would like to ask the person.

More steps are on the next card...

© Johnsen and Johnson, 1986

```
┌─────────────────────────────────────────────────────────┐
│  COLLECT            RESOURCE CARD                    39   │
│  INFORMATION                                             │
│                                                          │
│  INTERVIEW                                               │
│                                                          │
│  STEPS (continued):                                      │
│                                                          │
│  2.  During the interview                                │
│                                                          │
│   • When you meet the person, introduce yourself, shake hands and thank him/her for giving │
│     you the interview.                                   │
│                                                          │
│   • If you wish to tape record the interview, ask the person for permission. │
│                                                          │
│   • Ask the questions from the list, but don't limit yourself to the list.  If the person is talking │
│     about something of interest, ask follow-up questions.  Much of our most interesting │
│     information comes from spontaneous communication.    │
│                                                          │
│   • Be a good listener; look directly at the person.     │
│                                                          │
│   • Listen for clue words and phrases that tell you something important is coming. │
│                                                          │
│                 More steps are on the back...            │
│                                                          │
│                              © Johnson and Johnson, 1986 │
└─────────────────────────────────────────────────────────┘
```

```
┌─────────────────────────────────────────────────────────┐
│                                                    39b   │
│                                                          │
│  INTERVIEW                                               │
│                                                          │
│  STEPS (continued):                                      │
│                                                          │
│   • Take a few notes about important information.        │
│                                                          │
│   • Allow a few seconds of silent time after the person stops talking.  Allow time for the person to │
│     think through responses and perhaps add more information. │
│                                                          │
│   • Try to visualize or see pictures in you mind.        │
│                                                          │
│   • Keep to the time limit.  If you have told the person that the interview would be no more that │
│     thirty minutes, be sure to stop after thirty minutes.  If they want to spend more time, they can │
│     tell you.                                            │
│                                                          │
│   • When the interview is finished, thank the person again and express that he/she has been very │
│     helpful to you in your study.                        │
│                                                          │
│                 More steps are on the next card...       │
│                                                          │
│                              © Johnson and Johnson, 1986 │
└─────────────────────────────────────────────────────────┘
```

Procedure:

4. Take the students as necessary to the school library and show them how to find topics in the Card Catalogue.

5. Collect books and show the students how to skim books for information (*i.e.*, look for headings, topic sentences, chapter titles, table of contents, index, charts, etc.).

6. Teach interviewing skills to small groups or individuals as necessary (see **Resource Cards 38, 39, 40** and **Teacher Guide, Lesson 18** for interviewing).

7. Assign students the task of following up on at least one of the resource ideas.

8. Allow time for students to gather general information and read available material on the general topic. Designate an area for them to keep their collected materials together.

9. Plan a time to get back together to discuss the progress made and the information found.

NOTE: They may encounter roadblocks and dead ends. Let them know that that's okay. Many of our seemingly good ideas don't work, and we must keep trying to find information in other places. Through trial and error they will begin to understand the process of basic research.)

10. **ASSIGNMENT**: Assign a date by which students will need to have their final topic selected.

```
┌─────────────────────────────────────────────────────────┐
│  COLLECT            RESOURCE CARD                    40   │
│  INFORMATION                                             │
│                                                          │
│  INTERVIEW                                               │
│                                                          │
│  STEPS (continued):                                      │
│                                                          │
│  3.  After the interview                                 │
│                                                          │
│   • Review the notes and tape recording as soon as possible while the information is fresh on │
│     your mind.                                           │
│                                                          │
│   • Write the interview in paragraph form to include in the report. │
│                                                          │
│   • Write the interviewed person a thank you note telling how much you appreciate the time that │
│     was spent helping you with the research project.     │
│                                                          │
│   • If possible, send the person a copy of the report you write or invite him/her to view the │
│     product when you present it to the class.            │
│                                                          │
│                              © Johnson and Johnson, 1986 │
└─────────────────────────────────────────────────────────┘
```

LESSON 4. TOPIC ORGANIZATION: INTRODUCTION; DESCRIPTIONS

Concepts: 1. Organization
                   2. Description

Objective: The student will organize a topic using a network of descriptions.

Materials: 1. Student Booklet, page 7
                   2. Resource Card 5
                   3. Blank overhead or chalkboard

Evaluation: Is the student able to organize a topic using a network of descriptions?

(**Note for Group Independent Study:** If the students are working in a group on a single topic, place this topic on the chalkboard in Step 7 and complete the network together. If they have chosen different aspects of the same general topic area, follow the lessons and have the students develop a network alone or in small groups.)

Procedure:

1. Write on the overhead or chalkboard the words "Organization of a topic." Ask the students for examples of "organization."

2. Write their responses on the overhead or chalkboard.

3. Look at their examples and identify how they are alike and different.

4. Write a definition for *organization of a topic*, using these likenesses and differences or use the one listed in the **Student Booklet, page 7**. ("Organizing a topic means to arrange it in a way which will help you find specific questions to ask.")

5. Have students open their booklets to page 7.

6. Tell students that they will be selecting one or more of the ways to organize their topics.

NOTE: If this is the students' first independent studies, teach them how to use the description method only. It is the easiest method to use and is always included for topic definition.

7. Place the topic "animals" on the chalkboard. Tell the students that they will think of ways of organizing the topic by descriptions. Tell them that when they are describing a topic, they are telling how the examples within the topic are alike and/or different. Put these animal examples on the board: robin, cardinal, snake, frog, dog, cat, lizard, shark.

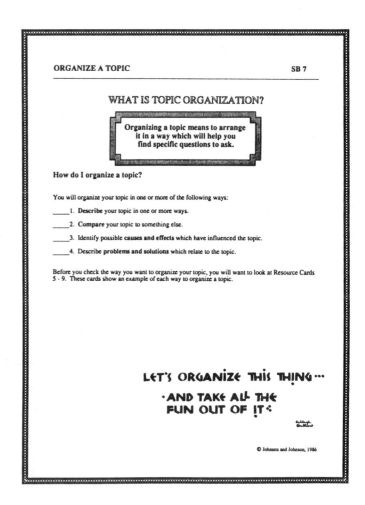

ORGANIZE A TOPIC   SB 7

WHAT IS TOPIC ORGANIZATION?

> Organizing a topic means to arrange it in a way which will help you find specific questions to ask.

How do I organize a topic?

You will organize your topic in one or more of the following ways:

_____ 1. Describe your topic in one or more ways.

_____ 2. Compare your topic to something else.

_____ 3. Identify possible causes and effects which have influenced the topic.

_____ 4. Describe problems and solutions which relate to the topic.

Before you check the way you want to organize your topic, you will want to look at Resource Cards 5 - 9. These cards show an example of each way to organize a topic.

LET'S ORGANIZE THIS THING···
·AND TAKE ALL THE
FUN OUT OF IT·

© Johnsen and Johnson, 1986

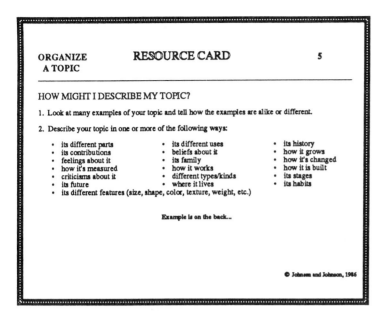

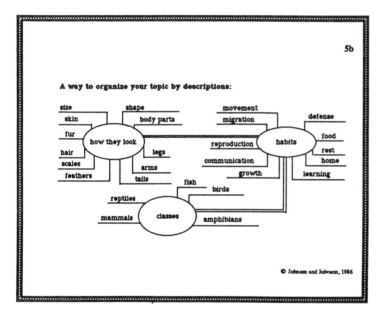

Procedure:

9. Ask the students to think to themselves for one minute about how these animals are alike and how they are different. After they have thought about these similarities and differences, have the students brainstorm their ideas. Some similarities might be: they all move; they all eat; they all reproduce; they all have skin covering; they all are colored; they all have mothers and fathers, *etc.* Some differences might be: they move in different ways, they eat different foods, they reproduce in different ways, they have different kinds of skin coverings, *etc.*

10. As the students brainstorm, place the students' ideas in a "web" or network fashion on the chalkboard. For example, if the students say, "they all move," write "they all move" on one line. If the students next say, "they all live on earth," draw a line from "they all move" to another space on the chalkboard and write, "they all live on earth." At the end of this process, you will have many lines, like a giant spiderweb, connecting many different brainstormed thoughts. They will have associated one idea with another (*e.g.*, appearance leads to appetite which leads to food which leads to vegetable, *etc.*).

11. When you are finished, be amazed with the students about the number of different areas that could be described about animals!

12. Now take these areas and classify them into higher order topics (see **Resource Card 5**). This classification process will assist them in developing questions in **Lesson 8, pages 17-18**.

13. Tell them that when they are studying a topic, they will always want to describe what they are studying first, but will probably not describe **everything** about the topic. This procedure will help them identify the areas they do want to describe. The next step is to ask questions about those areas.

14. **ASSIGNMENT:** Tell the students to develop a network about their topics. They might want to work with one another in small groups to brainstorm ideas.

LESSON 5. TOPIC ORGANIZATION: COMPARISONS

Concepts: Comparisons

Objective: The student will organize his/her topic by using comparisons.

Materials: 1. Student Booklet, page 7
                            2. Resource Card 6
                            3. Blank overhead or chalkboard

Evaluation: Is the student able to organize a topic by using comparisons?

(Note for Group Independent Study: If the students are working in a group on a single topic, place this topic on the chalkboard in Step 5 and complete the chart together. If they have chosen different aspects of the same general topic area, follow the lessons and have the students develop a chart alone or in small groups.)

Procedure:

1. Write on the overhead or chalkboard the word "comparison." Ask the students for general ways that they can compare one topic with another (see **Resource Card 6**):

   - how they look
   - how they are used
   - their histories
   - their futures
   - how people feel about them
   - how they grow and change

2. Write their responses on the overhead or chalkboard.

3. Look at their examples and identify how they are alike and different.

4. Write the definition for "comparison" using these likenesses and differences or the one listed on the **Resource Card 6**. ("Comparing a topic means to tell how it is the same or how it is different when it is compared to another description, a perfect model, or a rule.")

5. Place the topic "animals" on the chalkboard. Show the example of the "animals" organized by descriptions on the back of **Resource Card 6**.

6. Identify two kinds of animals that they would like to compare. They may compare topics that are very similar like chimpanzees with gorillas or very different topics like gorillas with lizards.

ORGANIZE A TOPIC   **RESOURCE CARD**   6

HOW MIGHT I COMPARE MY TOPIC?

1. Tell how your topic's description is the same or how it is different when it is compared to the description of another topic, a perfect model or a rule.

2. Compare your topic with something else in one or more of the following ways:

   - how their parts are different or the same
   - how their history is different or the same
   - how their growth is different or the same
   - how people's feelings about them are different or the same
   - how their uses are different or the same
   - how their features are different or the same
   - how any of your descriptions are different or the same

   Example is on the back...

   © Johnsen and Johnson, 1986

6b

A way to organize your topic by comparisons:

Comparison	Animals	
	Amphibians	Reptiles
1. Appearance		
2. Home		
3. Defense		
4. Food		
5. Growth		
6. Communication		

©Johnsen and Johnson, 1986

Procedure:

7. Ask the students to think to themselves for one minute about how they might compare the descriptions for each kind of animal. After they have thought about the descriptions, have the students brainstorm their ideas about how they could compare different descriptions.

8. Place the students' ideas on a chart as shown on the back of **Resource Card 6.**

9. When you are finished, count the number of different descriptions that could be compared!

10. Now have the students think about "perfect" models that would relate to the area of "animals." For example, the "perfect" pet, the "perfect" zoo, the "perfect" storybook animal, etc. Again, have the students brainstorm all of their "perfect" models.

11. Tell them that when they are comparing their topic or a description within their topic to a "perfect" model, they need to (1) describe the topic or description, (2) describe the "perfect" model, then (3) compare the two.

12. To practice have the students select one of their "perfect" models and describe its characteristics. Then have the students select an example of a "current" model. Finally, have the students compare the two.

13. **ASSIGNMENT:** Tell the students to develop a list of comparisons about their topic. They might want to work with one another in small groups to brainstorm ideas.

If I have succeeded in my inquiries more than others,
I owe it less to any superior strength of mind than to a habit of patient thinking.

I. Newton

LESSON 6. TOPIC ORGANIZATION: CAUSES AND EFFECTS

Concepts: 1. Causes
                   2. Effects
                   3. Changes

Objective: The student will organize a topic by using causes and effects.

Materials: 1. Student Booklet, page 7
                   2. Resource Card 7
                   3. Blank overhead or chalkboard

Evaluation: Is the student able to organize a topic by using causes and effects?

(Note for Group Independent Study: If the students are working in a group on a single topic, place this topic on the chalkboard in Step 6 and complete the chart together. If they have chosen different aspects of the same general topic area, follow the lessons and have the students develop a chart alone or in small groups.)

Procedure:

1. Write on the overhead or chalkboard the word "changes." Have the students give examples of changes.

2. Write their responses on the overhead or chalkboard.

3. Look at their examples and identify how they are alike and different.

4. Write the definition for "changes" using these likenesses and differences or the one listed on **Resource Card 7**. (A "change" is when a difference has happened or occurred.) Continue in this fashion with the words "causes" and "effects." ("Causes" are those things that happen before the "change" and may produce the change; "effects" are those things that happen after the "change" and are connected or related to the change.)

5. List the types of changes that might occur from **Resource Card 7** or from student responses. For example, changes from the past to the present, from the present to the future, in parts or structure, in usefulness, in beliefs about it, in its purpose, in its habits, *etc.*

6. Have the students brainstorm the changes that have occurred at home or at school since they were born (an example of a change from the past to the present). List these on the chalkboard or overhead. Repeat this process for each change listed in Step 5.

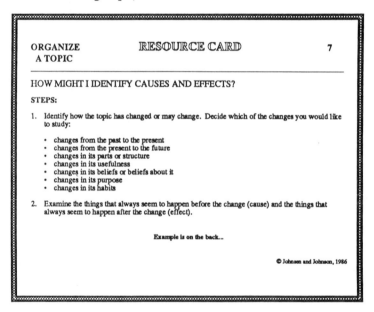

Procedure:

7. When they are finished, examine their "huge" list of changes.

8. Now have the students select one of their changes. If needed, use the evaluation process described on pages **TG 4** and **TG 5, Lesson 2**. Place this change between the words "causes" and "effects" as on **Resource Card 7**. List broad categories of possible "causes" and "effects" (*e.g.*, social causes and effects, economic causes and effects, educational causes and effects, familial causes and effects, etc.) and have the students brainstorm possible causes and effects under each category.

9. Talk about reasons which might be used in determining which causes and effects are "true" (*e.g.*, correlational research, number of resources which corroborate cause or effect, experts' opinions, experimentation, etc.).

10. **ASSIGNMENT**: Tell the students to develop lists of changes about their topic. If they have enough information they might also wish to list some POSSIBLE causes and/or effects. They might want to work with one another in small groups to brainstorm ideas.

You are today
where your thoughts
have brought you.
You will be tomorrow
where your thoughts
take you.

J. Allen

LESSON 7.   TOPIC ORGANIZATION: PROBLEMS AND SOLUTIONS

Concepts: 1. Problems
                   2. Solutions

Objective: The student will organize a topic by using problems and solutions.

Materials: 1. Student Booklet, page 7
                   2. Resource Cards 8, 9, 35
                   3. Blank overhead or chalkboard

Evaluation: Is the student able to organize a topic by using problems and solutions?

(**Note for Group Independent Study**: If the students are working in a group on a single topic, place this topic on the chalkboard in Step 6 and complete the chart together. If they have chosen different aspects of the same general topic area, follow the lessons and have the students develop a chart alone or in small groups.)

Procedure:

1. Write on the overhead or chalkboard the word "problems." Have the students give examples of problems. Write their responses on the overhead or chalkboard. Look at their examples and identify how they are alike and different.

2. Write the definition for "problems" using these likenesses and differences or the one listed on **Resource Card 8**. (A "problem" is a difficulty in which more than one solution is possible.) Continue in this fashion with the word "solution." ("Solutions" are those things that change or eliminate the problem.)

3. List the types of problems that might occur from **Resource Card 8** or from student responses. For example, differences between what is wanted and what is happening now, between what is happening now and what might happen in the future, between what is really happening and what is only imagined to be happening, *etc.*

4. Have the students brainstorm the problems that have occurred at home or at school since they were born.

5. When they are finished, examine their list of problems.

6. Now have the students select one of their problems. Place this problem on the chalkboard.

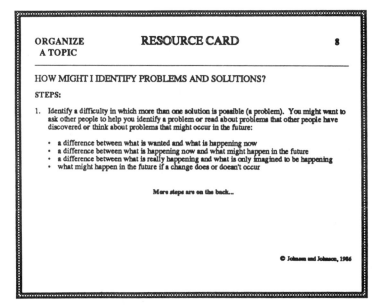

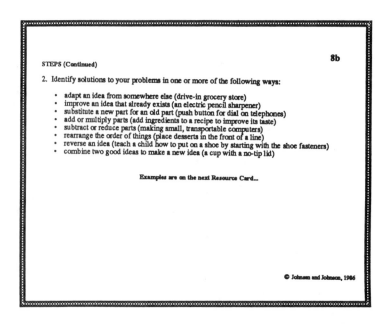

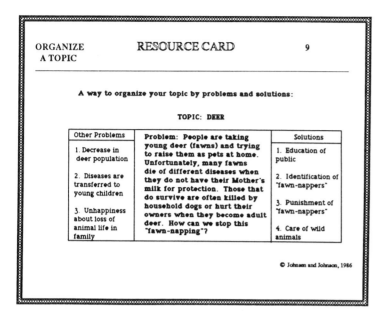

Procedure:

7. Think about related problems (other problems that might also occur if this problem is present). Identify the "big" problem. (If this problem were solved it would solve all of the other "little" problems). Write this problem on the board.

8. Now have the students break into small groups and identify possible solutions to the problem. Give each group ten minutes to brainstorm at least 20 solutions (see **Resource Card 9** for an example of a "big" problem, some related problems, and some related solutions).

9. When each group has 20 solutions. Place the word "SCAMPER" on the board. Tell them that they are going to "SCAMPER" and think of more solutions. Tell them that each letter in the word "SCAMPER" stands for a way of finding more solutions to the same problem. (See **Resource Card 35**).

10. Place the letter "S" on the board. Write the word "substitute" beside the letter. Tell the students to look at their solutions and substitute a *who* or a *what* in some of their solutions to produce at least five more solutions. Use one of the group's solutions to give them an example. Have the students substitute for two minutes.

11. Now place the letter "C" on the board. Write the word "combine" on the board. Tell the students to look at their solutions again and combine two or more of their solutions into one to produce at least five more solutions. Use one of the group's solutions to give them an example. Have the students combine for two more minutes.

12. Continue in this fashion using the SCAMPER techniques listed on **Resource Card 35**. Have the students count the number of solutions that their group generated and have them share their best solutions with the entire class.

13. Discuss the types of information that would be needed to make a decision about the best solution such as effectiveness, humaneness, efficiency, *etc.*

14. **ASSIGNMENT**: Tell the students to develop lists of problems about their topic.

LESSON 8. ASK "W" QUESTIONS

Concepts:	1. Good Study Questions 2. "W" Questions
Objective:	The student will be able to write six good study questions about a topic using "W" words.
Materials:	1. Resource Cards 10, 11 2. Student lists or networks from Lessons 4, 5, 6, and/or 7 (if completed) 3. Student Booklet, page 8 3. Blank overhead or chalkboard
Evaluation:	Given a topic and "W" words, is the student able to write at least six good study questions?

(Note for Group Independent Study: If the students are working as a group, complete each step using the topic that has been selected by the group.)

Procedure:

1. Write on the overhead or chalkboard the words "good study questions." Write these criteria for a good study question:

    *   It requires more than one answer.
    *   Two different people would not give the same answer.
    *   I would have the time to study it.
    *   I would be able to collect information.
    *   Others might find it useful or beneficial.

2. Have the students look at some examples of "good" and "poor" study questions in the **Student Booklet, page 8.** Have them evaluate which ones are "good" and "poor." (If you need more examples, look on the back of **Resource Card 10.**)

3. If the students learned about organizing a topic, have them look at their networks or lists and create questions using these descriptions, comparisons, causes, effects, problems, and/or solutions. If not, have the students simply tell questions that they could ask about their topic(s). Encourage them to ask both good and poor questions so the class can learn the difference. Have the class evaluate which ones are good study questions and which ones are not good study questions according to the criteria.

4. Now place the topic heading "Seals" (or the group topic) on the chalkboard or overhead. Under the heading, place the words "Who," "What," "When," "Where," "Why," and "How."

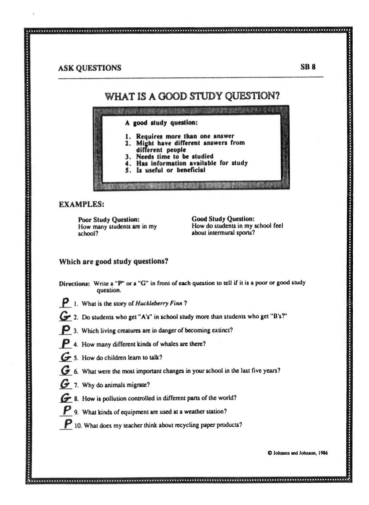

ASK QUESTIONS   **RESOURCE CARD**   **10**

HOW DO I KNOW IF I HAVE A GOOD STUDY QUESTION?

1. It requires more than one answer.
2. Two people would not give the same answer.
3. I would have the time to study it.
4. I would be able to collect information about it.
5. Others might find it useful or beneficial.

Examples are on the back...

© Johnsen and Johnson, 1986

10b

EXAMPLES:

POOR STUDY QUESTIONS:	GOOD STUDY QUESTIONS:
What color is an orange?	Why do wars occur?
Who invented the telephone?	How many kinds of insects are in my neighborhood?
How many students are in my class?	What is the relationship between grades and future achievement?
When was Hawaii admitted as a state?	Where do new ideas come from?

REMEMBER A GOOD STUDY QUESTION REQUIRES MORE THAN ONE ANSWER!

© Johnsen and Johnson, 1986

ASK QUESTIONS   **RESOURCE CARD**   **11**

"W" QUESTIONS and "H" QUESTIONS

Different beginning words help you write different types of questions. The words that are often used at the beginning of questions are these:

Who?	How much?
What?	How many?
When?	How long?
Where?	How far?
Why?	
What might happen if?	

Example is on the back...

© Johnsen and Johnson, 1986

Procedure:

5. Tell the students that these words are helpful in thinking of different kinds of information about their topics and will also help in asking questions.

6. Now write a question beside the word "Who." For example, "Who studies seals?" Have the students give another example. (If the students are using their own topics, have them use their networks and/or lists that they developed in "Organize a Topic" to provide additional stimulation for developing questions.)

7. Now write questions beside the word "What." For example, "What does a seal look like?" Have the students give another example. Continue in this fashion until there are several questions beside each word. (Use **Resource Card 11** to find more questions about seals.)

8. Examine all of the questions together and decide which ones are good study questions and which ones are not.

9. **ASSIGNMENT:** Tell the students to write "W" questions about their topic(s). If they do not know very much about their topic(s), they will want to look at some resources before they begin asking questions.

11b

EXAMPLES:

Topic: Seals

What does a seal look like?
Where do seals live?
How many different types of seals are there?
When do seals breed?
How do seals communicate?
Who studies seals?
Why are seals protected by treaties?
Why is there a disagreement over the hunting of seals?

© Johnsen and Johnson, 1986

LESSON 9.   ASK HIGHER LEVEL THINKING QUESTIONS

Concepts:
1. Little Thinking
2. More Thinking
3. Most Thinking

Objective: The student will be able to write study questions which include at least one "more" or "most" thinking question.

Materials:
1. Student Booklet, pages 9, 10, 11, 12, 13
2. Resource Cards 12, 13, 14
3. OH 2
4. "W" Questions from Lesson 8
5. Blank overhead or chalkboard

Evaluation: Given a topic and "W" questions, is the student able to classify these questions into types of thinking required and write at least one "more" or "most" thinking question?

(Note for Group Independent Study: If the students are working as a group, complete each step using the topic that has been selected by the group.)

Procedure:

NOTE: Students may find writing questions at higher levels of thinking a difficult task. Remember, plan extra time and many examples.

1. Write on overhead or chalkboard the words "little thinking."

2. Beside the words, write the following definition:

   "Questions which require 'little thinking' are those which can be answered by simply copying or redoing something that someone else has done."

   Tell the students that these types of questions **are needed** when they are first learning about their topics.

3. Write some example questions. You may want to use the questions listed on **Resource Card 12.**

4. Now have the students give some more examples of "little thinking" questions.

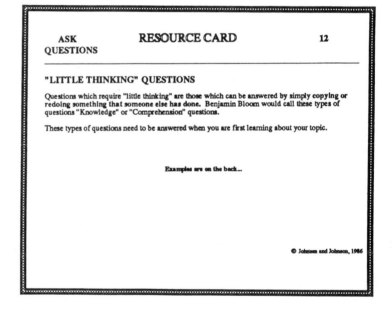

ASK QUESTIONS   **RESOURCE CARD**   12

"LITTLE THINKING" QUESTIONS

Questions which require "little thinking" are those which can be answered by simply copying or redoing something that someone else has done. Benjamin Bloom would call these types of questions "Knowledge" or "Comprehension" questions.

These types of questions need to be answered when you are first learning about your topic.

Examples are on the back...

© Johnson and Johnson, 1986

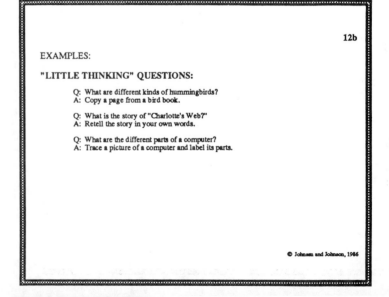

12b

EXAMPLES:

"LITTLE THINKING" QUESTIONS:

Q: What are different kinds of hummingbirds?
A: Copy a page from a bird book.

Q: What is the story of "Charlotte's Web?"
A: Retell the story in your own words.

Q: What are the different parts of a computer?
A: Trace a picture of a computer and label its parts.

© Johnson and Johnson, 1986

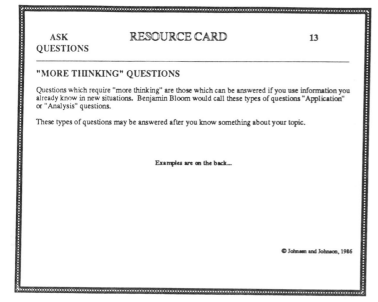

ASK QUESTIONS   RESOURCE CARD   13

"MORE THINKING" QUESTIONS

Questions which require "more thinking" are those which can be answered if you use information you already know in new situations. Benjamin Bloom would call these types of questions "Application" or "Analysis" questions.

These types of questions may be answered after you know something about your topic.

Examples are on the back...

© Johnsen and Johnson, 1986

13b

EXAMPLES:

"MORE THINKING" QUESTIONS:

Q: How do you classify birds?
A: Develop a game to teach others about how to classify birds.

Q: How do gerbils learn?
A: Plan an experiment to show how gerbils might learn.

Q: How do students feel about different subjects in school?
A: Have students describe their feelings during each subject. Put this information on a chart.

© Johnsen and Johnson, 1986

Procedure:

5. Write on the overhead or chalkboard the words "more thinking."

6. Beside the words, write the following definition:

   "Questions which require 'more thinking' are those which can be answered if you use the information you already know in new situations."

   Tell the students that these types of questions can be answered after they know something about their topics.

7. Write some example questions. You may want to use the questions listed on **Resource Card 13.**

8. Now have the students give some more examples of "more thinking" questions.

Procedure:

9. Write on overhead or chalkboard the words "most thinking."

10. Beside the words, write the following definition:

    "Questions which require 'most thinking' are those which can be answered by creating and/or evaluating new information."

    Tell the students that these types of questions are answered by new inventions, creations, or discoveries and require a lot of knowledge about their topics.

11. Write some example questions. You may want to use the questions listed on **Resource Card 14.**

12. Now have the students give some more examples of "most thinking" questions.

13. Put **OH2** on the overhead or distribute copies of the transparency to the class. Have them classify these questions as "little," "more," and "most" thinking.

ASK
QUESTIONS
RESOURCE CARD
14

"MOST THINKING" QUESTIONS

Questions which require the "most thinking" are those which can only be answered if you create and/or evaluate new information. Benjamin Bloom would call these types of questions "Synthesis" or "Evaluation" questions.

These types of questions are answered by new inventions, creations, or discoveries and require a lot of knowledge about your topic.

Examples are on the back...

© Johnsen and Johnson, 1986

14b

EXAMPLES:

"MOST THINKING" QUESTIONS:

Q: How might you develop a way to protect animals in urban areas?
A: Develop a plan to present to the City Council.

Q: How do you decide who should be president of the Student Council?
A: Conduct a survey at your school and develop a set of criteria for this position.

Q: How might I teach other students about computers?
A: Develop a set of learning games for the computer.

© Johnsen and Johnson, 1986

OH2

WHICH TYPE OF THINKING?

_____ How are daisies and bluebonnets alike? how are they different?

_____ How might you define the word "hero?"

_____ How might you plan a family reunion?

_____ Who were the first five presidents of the United States?

_____ Who do you think is the best writer in class? Why?

_____ What improvements could you make to the computer?

_____ What are the pro's and con's of rock music?

_____ How might you make a model to demonstrate your idea?

_____ Do you like living in this city? Why or why not?

104   © Johnsen and Johnson, 1986

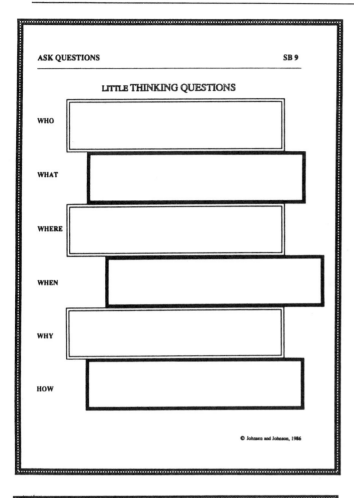

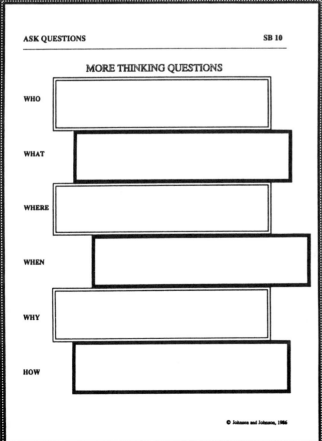

Procedure:

14. When you feel that the students understand how to classify questions, have them look at the **Student Booklets pages 9, 10, and 11.** Tell them to take their "W" questions (which they developed in Lesson 8) and write them on the correct pages. Give them time to add more questions. (You may not require them to write a question beside each word on each page.) Assist them in writing questions at a "more" and "most" thinking level or have them work in groups.

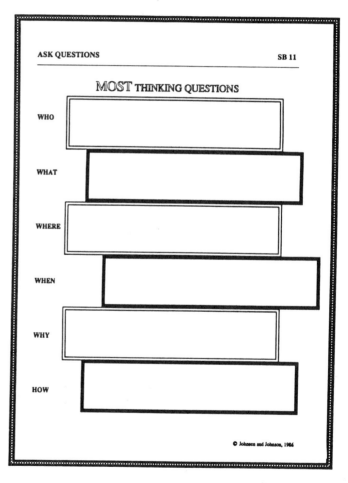

Procedure:

15. **ASSIGNMENT:** Have the students evaluate their questions using the **Student Booklets, pages 12 and 13.** Tell them that you would like for them to identify five questions to study including at least one "more" or "most" thinking question.

ASK QUESTIONS   SB 12

HOW DO I EVALUATE A STUDY QUESTION?

1. Select five questions to judge. Write these questions on the lines by the numbers.

2. Think of some reasons (criteria) by which you will judge your questions. For example, is the question of use or benefit to someone? Is the question interesting to me? Will I be able to find information about it?

3. Decide on three criteria and write them on the lines at the top of the chart by "A," "B," and "C."

4. Look at the first reason (criterion A). Put a "5" in the box next to the question that best fits criterion A. Put a "4" next to the question that is next best. Do the same with the numbers "3," "2," and "1." Follow the same process with the second reason (criterion B) and the third reason (criterion C).

5. Add the numbers next to each question and put the sum in the *Total* box. The highest total may be your best question to study.

EXAMPLE:

QUESTION EVALUATION CHART

C. The question requires the most thinking.

CRITERIA   B. The question will be most beneficial to others in the future.

A. The question is the most interesting to me.

QUESTIONS	A	B	C	TOTAL
1. How might I develop a way to protect endangered wildlife?				
2. How are birds' and mammals' habits alike and different?				
3. In what ways are plant and animal development the same or different?				
4. Do animals and humans develop communication systems in the same way?				
5. What might be a good way to evaluate zoos?				

adapted from Texas Future Problem Solving

© Johnson and Johnson, 1986

ASK QUESTIONS   SB 13

QUESTION EVALUATION CHART

Directions: Follow the example on SB 12. Write the reasons you might develop a study question beside Criteria A, B, and C. List five study questions on the lines below. Read criterion A and put a "5" beside the question that best matches that reason. Put a "4" by the next best question, and so on to "1." Rank questions using Criteria B and C in the same way.

C. _____

CRITERIA   B. _____

A. _____

QUESTIONS	A	B	C	TOTAL
1.				
2.				
3.				
4.				
5.				

adapted from Texas Future Problem Solving

I HAVE A
THEORY
THAT IT'S
IMPOSSIBLE
TO PROVE
ANYTHING

BUT
I CAN'T
PROVE
IT

© Johnson and Johnson, 1986

LESSON 10. IDENTIFY AND SEQUENCE QUESTIONS FOR STUDY

Concepts: 1. Question sequence
                                  2. Outlining

Objective: The student will be able to identify and sequence questions for study.

Materials: 1. Student Booklet, pages 2 and 3
                                  2. Blank overhead or chalkboard
                                  3. Questions from Teacher Guide, Lesson 8 or 9
                                  4. Teacher Guide, Lesson 22, 68-72
                                  5. Resource Card 60

Evaluation: Given a topic and questions, is the student able to identify good study questions and organize them into a sequence for study?

(**Note for Group Independent Study:** If the students are working as a group, use the selected group topic, beginning with Step 2).

Procedure:

1. Have the students tell which questions they decided to study (see **Teacher Guide, Lessons 8 or 9**).

2. If the students are studying different topics, write the questions selected by **one student** for his/her topic on the chalkboard or overhead. If not, use the group topic.

3. Tell the students that they are going to help organize these questions into a sequence for study. Tell them that to organize the questions, they need to group the questions into categories, then arrange them in a sequence.

4. In grouping the questions into categories have the students look at how the questions are alike and how they are different. For example, some of the questions may relate to how the topic looks, others may relate to how the topic is used, *etc*.

5. After the categories are identified and the questions are grouped, have the students think of possible ways to sequence the categories (*e.g.*, beginning to end, birth to death, developmental, historical, easy to hard, description to use, *etc*.).

6. Arrange the questions in different sequences, putting them in an outline form (see **Teacher Guide, Lesson 22 and Resource Card 60** for outlining information).

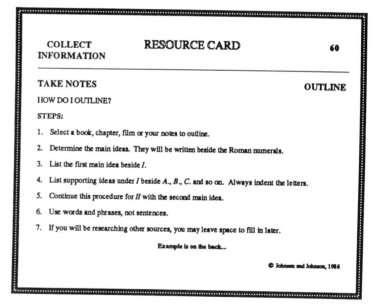

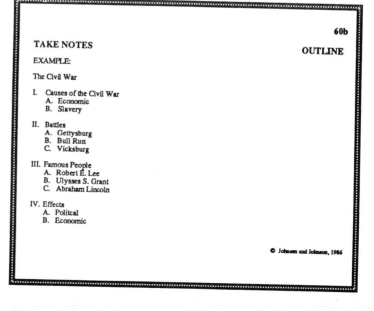

Procedure:

7. Let the student who identified a topic in Step 2 or the class decide which sequence to use. Have this student or the class write the sequence on the back of the Independent Study Plan(s) (see **Student Booklet, pages 2 and 3**).

8. Repeat this same procedure with other students' questions until all students understand how to organize and sequence their questions for study.

9. **ASSIGNMENT:** Have the students identify and sequence their questions for study.

All the deep and true joys of the world All the splendor and the mystery Are within our reach.

E. Heminyway

LESSON 11. INTRODUCTION TO STUDY METHOD

Concepts:	1. Study Method 2. Different Study Methods
Objective:	The student will be able to select a study method which matches the study question(s).
Materials:	1. Student Booklet, page 14 2. Resource Cards 15 to 31 3. Blank overhead or chalkboard
Evaluation:	Given a topic and questions, is the student able to follow the steps of a study method which matches the study questions?

(Note for Group Independent Study: Select and introduce the method which best matches the group's questions. If no one method appears to match the questions, follow the procedure listed below with the entire group.)

Procedure:

NOTE: With younger students you may decide to select a study method for them and show them the steps as they are needed. If you do, omit these lessons on Study Method.

1. Have the students look in the **Student Booklets, page 14.**

2. Read the definition at the top of the page. Tell them scientists follow certain steps when they study a question or a problem. The study method that is selected depends upon the type(s) of question that is asked.

3. Tell them to think about their questions as you describe different study methods. At the end of your discussion, tell them that you will ask them to identify a method of study.

4. Write on the overhead or chalkboard these headings: *Name, Methods, Questions.*

NOTE: You may decide to only discuss certain methods that you want the students to use during this particular independent study.

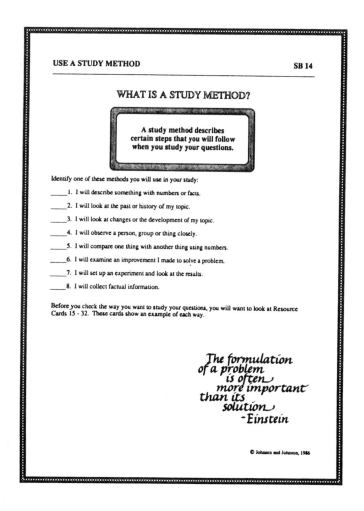

USE A STUDY METHOD   SB 14

WHAT IS A STUDY METHOD?

A study method describes certain steps that you will follow when you study your questions.

Identify one of these methods you will use in your study:

_____ 1. I will describe something with numbers or facts.

_____ 2. I will look at the past or history of my topic.

_____ 3. I will look at changes or the development of my topic.

_____ 4. I will observe a person, group or thing closely.

_____ 5. I will compare one thing with another thing using numbers.

_____ 6. I will examine an improvement I made to solve a problem.

_____ 7. I will set up an experiment and look at the results.

_____ 8. I will collect factual information.

Before you check the way you want to study your questions, you will want to look at Resource Cards 15 - 32. These cards show an example of each way.

The formulation of a problem is often more important than its solution
-Einstein

© Johnson and Johnson, 1986

Procedure:

5. Read the first statement, "I will describe something with numbers or facts." Write on the overhead or chalkboard "**Describe Topic**." Next to this title write: *surveys, questionnaires, interviews, observations, test scores, records*. Tell them that these are methods that are often used in describing a topic with numbers or facts. Now write two example questions, "In our school what is the attitude toward homework? On the average how much television is watched daily and/or weekly by students in our classroom?" Describe how these questions would be studied using the steps on **Resource Cards 16 and 17**. If any of the students think that they have questions that would be studied using this approach, place them with the other questions.

USE A
STUDY METHOD   **RESOURCE CARD**   16

HOW DO I DESCRIBE SOMETHING WITH NUMBERS OR FACTS?

STEPS:

1. Ask a question that can be answered with numbers or facts about your topic.

2. Decide if you are going to use information that is already known or get new information.

3. You can find old information in books, magazines, newspapers, encyclopedias, films, filmstrips, old records, movies, TV shows, etc.

4. You can get new information by doing interviews, surveys or experiments.

5. Develop a form to collect your data (i.e., numbers, information).

More steps are on the back...

© Johnsen and Johnson, 1986

USE A
STUDY METHOD   **RESOURCE CARD**   17

EXAMPLE OF HOW TO DESCRIBE SOMETHING WITH NUMBERS OR FACTS:

STEPS:

1. How many students in our school have pets? What kind of pets do they have?

2. Decide on the definition of a "pet." Identify the kinds of pets that you will include in the survey. Decide if you will include all of the students in the school or just select a sample.

3. Call the Humane Society to see if they have ever conducted a pet survey and if they might have suggestions of questions that would be interesting to include. Read about pets to make sure that you have included all of the necessary information.

4. Develop a survey to collect the information.

More steps are on the back...

© Johnsen and Johnson, 1986

16b

STEPS (continued):

6. If you are collecting new information, you will want to make sure that your information is objective. To make sure your information is objective, identify persons that represent your population and identify an observation or data collection method that tries to collect non-biased information.

7. Gather the information.

8. Identify what information is based on facts and what is based on opinion.

9. Summarize your notes.

10. Present your information to other people.

Example is on the next Resource Card...

© Johnsen and Johnson, 1986

17b

STEPS (continued):

5. Identify the students in school who will participate in the survey. Ask if they will be willing to participate. Find a time to ask the questions.

6. Ask each student the questions on the survey.

7. Summarize the information. Identify the number of students who own pets. Identify the different kinds of pets. Identify differences between boys and girls, between grade levels, and between ages.

8. Share the results with participating classes.

© Johnsen and Johnson, 1986

Procedure:

6. Read the next statement, "I will look at the past or history of my topic." Write on the overhead or chalkboard "**Describe History.**" Next to this title write: *interviews with primary sources, letters, notes from historical books or records.* Tell them that these are methods that are often used in describing the history of a topic. Now write two example questions, "How did the different schools in our town get their names? What is the history of the 'Rock and Roll' movement?" Describe how these questions would be studied using the steps on **Resource Cards 18 and 19.** If any of the students think that they have questions that would be studied using this approach, place them with the other questions.

USE A
STUDY METHOD   **RESOURCE CARD**   18

HOW DO I LOOK AT THE PAST OR HISTORY OF A TOPIC?

STEPS:

1. Ask a question that can be answered by looking at the past or history of the topic.

2. Look for both *primary* and *secondary* sources. In primary sources the author has directly observed the historical event. In secondary sources the author reports the observations of others.

3. You can find information from:

    *   people who observed the historical event
    *   historians at colleges and universities
    *   historical societies
    *   museums
    *   old documents, old records
    *   books
    *   magazines
    *   newspapers
    *   encyclopedias
    *   films, filmstrips
    *   movies
    *   TV shows

4. Take notes from the resources.

More steps are on the back...

© Johnsen and Johnson, 1986

USE A
STUDY METHOD   **RESOURCE CARD**   19

AN EXAMPLE OF HOW TO LOOK AT THE PAST OR HISTORY OF A TOPIC:

STEPS:

1. How did the different schools in our town get their names?

2. Call the principals of the different schools. Identify people who are living, who were either at the school building when it was dedicated or know the person or place for whom the school was named (primary sources).

3. Go to the library and to the newspaper. Find articles and/or stories about the persons and/or places for whom the schools were named (secondary sources).

4. Take notes from the secondary resources. Interview the primary sources.

More steps are on the back...

© Johnsen and Johnson, 1986

18b

STEPS (continued):

5. Examine the resources and your notes. Make sure that yhr resources are authentic: Would the author have a motive or a bias to exaggerate, distort or overlook information?

6. Decide which information is based on facts and which information is based on opinion.

7. Summarize the notes.

8. Present the information to other people. Be sure to include the names of all of the resources you used and tell how you decided whether or not they were authentic.

Example is on the next Resource Card...

© Johnsen and Johnson, 1986

19b

STEPS (continued):

5. Examine the interviews and your notes. Identify those persons who might tend to exaggerate information or who might be biased in some way.

6. Decide which information is based on facts and which information is based on opinion.

7. Summarize your notes. Identify how school names are often chosen. Identify the number of schools who were named after school leaders, community leaders, historical people, *etc.*

8. Present the information to other people. Be sure to include the names of all of the resources you used and tell how you decided whether or not they were authentic.

© Johnsen and Johnson, 1986

Procedure:

7. Read the next statement, "I will look at changes or the development of my topic." Write on the overhead or chalkboard **"Describe Development."** Next to this title write: *observations, questionnaires, tests, interviews, letters, library research.* Tell them that these are methods that are often used in describing the development of a topic. Now write two example questions, "What are my classmates' attitudes toward school throughout this year? Do they change? Do they remain the same?" Describe how these questions would be studied using the steps on **Resource Cards 20 and 21.** If any of the students think that they have questions that would be studied using this approach, place them with the other questions.

USE A STUDY METHOD   **RESOURCE CARD**   **20**

HOW DO I LOOK AT CHANGES OR THE DEVELOPMENT OF MY TOPIC?

STEPS:

1. Ask about a change or the development of the topic over time.

2. Examine how other people have looked at change or development of the topic in the past.

3. You can find how others have looked at change by:
   - interviewing experts
   - writing letters to people who are interested in the topic
   - reading books, magazines, journals, newspapers, encyclopedias.

4. Design a way that you will look at the change or development of the topic.

More steps are on the back...

© Johnsen and Johnson, 1986

USE A STUDY METHOD   **RESOURCE CARD**   **21**

AN EXAMPLE OF HOW TO LOOK AT THE DEVELOPMENT OF MY TOPIC:

STEPS:

1. What are my classmates' attitudes toward school throughout this year? Do they change? Do they remain the same?

2. Ask your teacher how other people have looked at attitudes.

3. Interview or write letters to educators at colleges and universities. Look in magazines and journals to see how others have looked at attitudes.

4. Define attitude. Identify the opinions you will want to collect. Design a form to measure these attitudes.

More steps are on the back...

© Johnsen and Johnson, 1986

20b

STEPS (continued):

5. Some ways to study change might be:
   - to give a test or questionnaire at the beginning and end of an activity and look at the differences
   - to observe something every day and graph or chart the information

6. Collect the data.

7. Summarize the data.

8. Present the information to other people. Be sure to include how others have observed changes in the topic, how you decided to observe changes and the results of what you observed.

Example is on the next Resource Card...

© Johnsen and Johnson, 1986

21b

STEPS (continued):

5. With your teacher decide on the same time each day that you will collect the data. Explain the form to your classmates.

6. Collect the data.

7. Summarize the data.
   - Did the attitudes change from the beginning of the year to the end of the year?
   - Did the attitudes change according to the day?
   - Did the attitudes change depending upon what was being studied?
   - Were there differences between boys and girls?

8. Present the results to the class. Be sure to include how others have observed attitudes and how you decided to observe attitudes.

© Johnsen and Johnson, 1986

Procedure:

8. Read the next statement, "I will observe a person, group or thing closely." Write on the overhead or chalkboard "**Case Study**." Next to this title write: *interviews, observations, tape recordings, notes.* Tell them that these are methods that are often used in observing a person, group or thing closely. Now write two example questions, "How does a principal spend his/her time during the school day? What are the backgrounds of teenage drug abusers?" Describe how these questions would be studied using the steps on **Resource Cards 22 and 23.** If any of the students think that they have questions that would be studied using this approach, place them with the other questions.

USE A
STUDY METHOD   **RESOURCE CARD**   22

HOW DO I OBSERVE A PERSON, GROUP OR SOMETHING CLOSELY?

STEPS:

1. Ask a question that requires you to observe a person, group or something closely.

2. Examine how other people have looked at the person, group, or thing.

3. You can find how others have looked at the person, group or thing by:

   • interviewing experts
   • writing letters to people who are interested in the topic
   • reading books, magazines, journals or newspapers

4. If you are going to observe a person or group, find a person(s) who is willing to let you observe him/her. If you are going to observe a place or thing, locate it and get permission to observe it.

More steps are on the back...

© Johnson and Johnson, 1986

USE A
STUDY METHOD   **RESOURCE CARD**   23

EXAMPLE OF HOW TO OBSERVE A PERSON CLOSELY:

STEPS:

1. How does a principal spend his/her time during the school day?

   • read books that describe what principals do
   • ask different principals what they do
   • interview people at colleges who teach principals what to do

2. Identify when you will observe and how you will collect information. You will probably want to use notes as well as a tape recorder.

3. Find a principal who is willing to let you observe him/her. Ask the principal what he/she does during a "typical" school day.

4. Design a form that you will use in taking notes. You will want to have a way of recording the time and place of the principal's activity.

More steps are on the back...

© Johnson and Johnson, 1986

22b

STEPS (continued):

5. Design a way to observe the person, group or thing. Decide how long you will observe, how you will take notes (in a journal? in an interview? on a tape recorder? on cards?).

6. Collect the data by observing the person, group or thing.

7. Summarize the data.

8. Present the information to other people. Tell them why you decided to observe this person, group or thing, how you conducted your observation and what you learned.

Example is on the next Resource Card...

© Johnson and Johnson, 1986

23b

STEPS (continued):

6. Observe the principal over a period of time. His/her activity will probably change from day to day and from week to week.

7. Look at the notes and summarize the data.

   • name the different types of activities
   • find the average amount of time that is spent on various activities

8. Present the information to the principal, teacher and classmates. Tell them how you collected the information.

© Johnson and Johnson, 1986

Procedure:

9. Read the next statement, "I will compare one thing with another thing using numbers." Write on the overhead or chalkboard "**Correlation Study.**" Next to this title write: *interviews, observations, tape recordings, notes, tests, surveys, readings, census information.* Tell them that these are methods that are often used in comparing one thing with another thing using numbers. Now write two example questions, "Is there a relationship between the number of study hours at home and grades? Is there a relationship between grades in elementary school and grades in junior high (middle school)?" Describe how these questions would be studied using the steps on **Resource Cards 24 and 25.** If any of the students think that they have questions that would be studied using this approach, place them with the other questions.

24b

STEPS (continued):

5. Collect the data.

6. Put the data about one item on a line graph. Put the data about the other item on a separate line graph or a separate line on the same graph. Compare the two items.

7. Analyze the data on the graph:

- If the two lines go up or down in the same way (*i.e.*, are parallel), the items are related. When one item occurs, the other will probably happen.
- If one line goes down and one line goes up, the items are *inversely* related. When one item occurs, the other will probably *not* happen.
- If the lines don't look like the described ways, the items are probably not related.

8. Share the information with other people.

© Johnson and Johnson, 1986

USE A STUDY METHOD   **RESOURCE CARD**   24

HOW DO I COMPARE ONE THING WITH ANOTHER THING USING NUMBERS?

STEPS:

1. Ask a question that requires you to compare one thing with another thing using numbers.

2. Describe each thing that you are going to compare. Look at how others have described these things and how they have measured or studied them.

3. Decide what or who will be in the study. Remember to select a sample that represents the general population and is not biased.

4. Decide how you will measure each thing that you are going to compare:

- Will you look at tests?
- Will you observe how they grow?
- Will you get information from newspapers?

More steps are on the back...

© Johnson and Johnson, 1986

USE A STUDY METHOD   **RESOURCE CARD**   25

EXAMPLE OF HOW TO COMPARE ONE THING WITH ANOTHER THING:

STEPS:

1. Is there a relationship between the number of study hours at home and grades?

2. Look at how others have studied this relationship. Ask students and teachers in your school. Ask experts at local colleges and universities.

3. Define what you mean by "study hours" and "grades."

4. Decide what subject area you will study and who will be in your study.

5. Decide how you will measure "study hours" and "grades." Develop a form that the participants can use at home and find a satisfactory way to collect test grades.

6. Find the students who are willing to participate in your study. Have them collect the data for one semester.

More steps are on the back...

© Johnson and Johnson, 1986

25b

STEPS (continued):

7. Examine the students who made good grades and the students who made poor grades.

- Chart the number of hours the students who made good grades studied at home.
- Chart the number of hours the students who made poor grades studied at home.

8. Compare the grades with hours studied.

- If the two lines go up or down in the same way (*i.e.*, are parallel), the things are related. When one thing happens, the other will probably happen.
- If one line goes down and one line goes up, the things are inversely related. When one thing happens, the other will probably not happen.
- If the lines don't look like the described ways, the things are probably not related.

9. Share the information with other people.

© Johnson and Johnson, 1986

Procedure:

10. Read the next statement, "I will examine an improvement I made to solve a problem." Write on the overhead or chalkboard, "**Action Study**." Next to this title write: *interviews, observations, training programs, experiments, tests, surveys, readings*. Tell them that these are methods that are often used to make and examine an improvement that is made to solve a problem. Now write two example questions, "How can we reduce the noise and trash in the cafeteria? How can I improve my test scores in mathematics?" Describe how these questions would be studied using the steps on **Resource Cards 26 and 27**. If any of the students think that they have questions that would be studied using this approach, place them with the other questions.

USE A
STUDY METHOD   **RESOURCE CARD**   26

HOW DO I EXAMINE AN IMPROVEMENT I MADE TO SOLVE A PROBLEM?

STEPS:

1. Ask a question that can be answered by looking at an improvement.

2. Identify a problem that needs to be solved.

3. Find information about how others have solved this problem:

   - experts at colleges and universities
   - businesses, Chambers of Commerce
   - books, magazines, newspapers, journals
   - T. V. shows

4. Take notes from the resource.

5. Decide in what situation and how you want to solve the problem.

More steps are on the back...

© Johnsen and Johnson, 1986

USE A
STUDY METHOD   **RESOURCE CARD**   27

EXAMPLE OF HOW TO EXAMINE AN IMPROVEMENT MADE TO SOLVE A PROBLEM:

STEPS:

1. How can we reduce the noise and trash in the cafeteria?

2. Find information about how others have solved this problem:

   - other schools
   - principals
   - teachers
   - students
   - Student Councils

3. Take notes from the resource.

4. Develop a plan to reduce the noise and trash. For example, each class could earn points for having a quiet and clean area. These points could be traded in for eating lunch outside, having extra time before returning to class, having others clean their area, *etc*.

More steps are on the back...

© Johnsen and Johnson, 1986

26b

STEPS (continued):

6. Decide how you will measure whether or not your improvement changes the problem. For example, you may want to test it at the beginning and at the end, or you may want to graph changes every day.

7. Get permission from everyone who will be involved in the study.

8. Collect the data.

9. Record and analyze the results.

10. Present the information to other people.

© Johnsen and Johnson, 1986

27b

STEPS (continued):

5. Decide how you will measure whether or not the improvement changes the noise and trash level. Define "noise" and "trash" and develop forms to measure each.

6. Get permission from everyone who will be involved in your study.

7. Collect the data before you implement the plan. Implement the plan. Collect data after you implement the plan.

8. Compare the "noise" and "trash" level before and after you have implemented the plan.

9. Present the information to the participants. See how they like the new plan.

© Johnsen and Johnson, 1986

Procedure:

11. Read the next statement, "I will set up an experiment and look at the results." Write on the overhead or chalkboard, "**Experimental Study.**" Next to this title write: *interviews, observations, training programs, treatments, tests, surveys, readings.* Tell them that these are methods that are often used to set up an experiment and look at the results." Now write this example question, "Does memorizing spelling lists from a spelling book help spell similar words in other spelling lists and in writing sentences?" Describe how this question would be studied using the steps on **Resource Cards 28, 29, and 30.** If any of the students think that they have questions that would be studied using this approach, place them with the other questions.

28b

STEPS (continued):

6. Select a research design (see the next Resource Card).

   - Assign parts of the sample to different groups.
   - Select or design the instruments that you are going to use to measure the variables.
   - Design the treatment if needed.
   - Identify how you are going to collect the data.

7. Conduct the experiment.

8. Summarize the data. Use graphs, charts, and/or tables to show the data.

9. Present the information to other people.

© Johnson and Johnson, 1986

USE A   **RESOURCE CARD**   **29**
STUDY METHOD

WHAT ARE SOME DIFFERENT RESEARCH DESIGNS?

STEPS:

1. Experimental Group(s) and Control Group(s)

   - In this design select two groups.
   - Give both groups a pretest and both groups a post test.
   - Give only one group the treatment (*e.g.* the experimental group).
   - Then compare the differences between groups on the post test to see if the treatment made a change in the experimental group.

   This design can be varied by adding more experimental groups or more control groups. In this way, more treatments or more control variables can be tested.

   Another design is on the back...

© Johnson and Johnson, 1986

USE A   **RESOURCE CARD**   **28**
STUDY METHOD

HOW DO I SET UP AN EXPERIMENT AND LOOK AT THE RESULTS?

STEPS:

1. Ask a question that requires you to look at one thing (*i.e.*, a variable) that may be changing while you try to control other things (*i.e.*, variables).

2. Describe each variable that is going to be in the experiment.

   - Identify the "dependent" variable, the change you are examining.
   - Identify the "independent" variables, the things that may be influencing the change.

3. Look at how others have described these variables and how they have measured or studied them.

4. Decide what or who will be in the study. Remember to select a sample that represents the general population and is not biased.

5. Decide how you will measure the variables. For example, will you look at tests? Will you observe how they grow? Will you get information from people?

More steps are on the back...

© Johnson and Johnson, 1986

29b

STEPS (continued):

2. Time-Series Design with One or More Groups

   - In this design select one or more groups.
   - Give the group(s) several tests over a period of time. In this way you can eliminate the possibility that the change was influenced by time only.
   - Then administer a treatment.
   - After the treatment, give several post tests over a period of time. Again, you can see the effect of time on the treatment.

There are many more research designs, ask your teacher, talk to researchers or look in different resources for more ideas.

© Johnson and Johnson, 1986

Procedure:

12. Read the next statement, "I will collect factual information." Write on the overhead or chalkboard, "**Every Study.**" Next to this title write "any of the above methods." Tell them that for any question studied, they should collect factual information. Describe how factual information may be collected by using the steps on **Resource Card 31.** (You may want to compare facutal information with opinions.)

13. **ASSIGNMENT:** Tell the students to select one or more study methods that match their questions.

USE A
STUDY METHOD   **RESOURCE CARD**   30

EXAMPLE OF HOW TO SET UP AN EXPERIMENT:

STEPS:

1. Does memorizing spelling lists from a spelling book help in spelling similar words in other spelling lists and in writing sentences?

2. Writing similar words spelled correctly both in spelling lists and in writing sentences are the "dependent" variables. Memorizing spelling lists is the "independent" variable.

3. Look at how others have described spelling "correctly" and how they have measured or studied it.

4. Decide which students will be in the study. Select groups that are equal in ability as spellers. Have one group that doesn't see the book and doesn't memorize spelling lists; have another group that does memorize spelling lists. If you have enough students (10 in each group), you could have other groups as well. For example, one that has a different spelling book and never sees the words and one that plays games with the spelling words.

More steps are on the back...

© Johnson and Johnson, 1986

USE A
STUDY METHOD   **RESOURCE CARD**   31

HOW DO I COLLECT FACTUAL INFORMATION?

STEPS:

1. Ask a question.

2. Identify resources that you will need to answer the question. If possible, ask other people about good resources who may be interested in your topic.

2. Gather the information from more than one resource.

3. Take notes from the resources.

4. Summarize the information.

More steps are on the back...

© Johnson and Johnson, 1986

30b

STEPS (continued):

5. Decide how you will measure "similar words in spelling tests and in writing sentences" and "spelling lists." You might decide to use the spelling lists and sentences from the spelling book with one group having access to the book and the other group not having access to the book.

6. Identify how you are going to collect the data.

7. Conduct the experiment for at least three weeks.

8. Summarize the data. Show the number of words spelled correctly by each group on a graph and/or on a chart.

9. Present the information to the class.

© Johnson and Johnson, 1986

31b

STEPS (continued):

5. Identify the information that is factual and the information that is opinion. You will find that factual information is repeated in various resources, while opinions may be different in various resources.

FACT: Texas is the second largest state in the United States.
OPINION: I believe that Texas is the nicest state to live in.

6. Share the information with others.

© Johnson and Johnson, 1986

LESSON 12. NONBIASED SAMPLES

Concepts: 1. Nonbiased Sample
                   2. Sampling Error
                   3. Random Sample
                   4. Bias

Objective: The student will be able to select a nonbiased sample by using a random sampling procedure.

Materials: 1. Questionnaire about study and TV hours (HO 1, page 114 in the Teacher's Guide)
                   2. Completed questionnaires from other classes in the school (see Steps 12-15 of this lesson)
                   3. Resource Card 32
                   4. Blank overhead or chalkboard

Evaluation: Given a topic and questions, is the student able to follow the steps of a study method and use a random sampling procedure to select a nonbiased sample?

(**Note for Group Independent Study:** Follow the procedure listed below with the entire group.)

Procedure:

NOTE: With younger students you may decide to select a study method for them and show them the steps as they are needed. If you do, you will omit these lessons on Study Method.

1. Write the word "sample" on the overhead or chalkboard.

2. Say to the students, "If you were to sample some cake batter, what would the word "sample" mean? Write their definitions on the board. Now say, "If you were to take a sample of students from this class, what would the word 'sample' mean then? " Write their definitions on the board.

3. Use one of the student's definitions or say to the students, "When we sample, we are selecting a smaller amount of persons or things from a possibly larger amount of persons or things (called a population)."

4. Write on the chalkboard or overhead some of these examples: *some books about our topic, a class from an entire school, a telephone poll about your favorite TV show, one kind of plant.* Ask the students for more examples. List these.

5. Tell (or ask the students) the reasons for selecting a sample instead of using the entire population: saves time, can't use entire population, can't find entire population, can't get permission to use the entire population, saves money, no access to computer for large data analysis.

6. Say to the students, "The sample should be as representative or as similar to the entire population as possible. However, it is never identical. The difference between the sample and the population is called the **'sampling error.'** (**Write these words on the board**). As a researcher and scientist, you will want this error to be as small as possible for these reasons: (**Write these reasons on the board.**)

    A. *You can generalize your research to other samples.*

    B. *You can compare two samples and say that differences in the two samples are a result of what you are studying and not a result of the samples being different."*

```
HO1
                    QUESTIONNAIRE

_____

#_____

Fill in the information below:

1. _____Boy _____Girl

2. _____Birthday

3. _____Grade


_____

Check only one line which is nearest to the amount of time you spend each
evening watching television and doing homework:

4. The approximate amount of time I study each night:

        ____less than 30 minutes
        ____30 minutes to one hour
        ____more than one hour
        ____more than two hours
        ____more than three hours

5. The approximate amount of time I watch T.V. each night:

        ____less than 30 minutes
        ____30 minutes to one hour
        ____more than one hour
        ____more than two hours
        ____more than three hours
        ____I don't have a T.V.

_____

Now complete each statement below with one answer:

6. My favorite subject in school is _____.

7. My favorite T. V. show is _____.


                    114              © Johnson and Johnson, 1986
```

Procedure:

7. Give some examples for generalization:

   Example 1: This plant is like all of the other plants. My experiment with this plant will have the same effect as it does with all the other plants just like it.
   Example 2: This class is like all of the other classes in the school. Its opinions will be like the opinions of the entire school.
   Example 3: This soda is like all of the other sodas. The way that it tastes will be like all of the other sodas just like it.
   Example 4: This book about tennis is like all of the other books about tennis. What it says will be what all of the other books say.

   Have the students add to the list of generalizations using their topics or the group topic.

8. Give some examples of comparing two samples:

   Example 1: These boxes of cake mix are alike. The final cakes will indicate differences in the cook not differences in the boxes of cake mix
   Example 2: The students in these two classes are alike. Final spelling test scores will indicate differences in their performances on the tests not simply differences in the students.

   Again have the students add to the list of comparisons using their topics or the group topic.

9. Tell the students that they are going to learn how to get nonbiased samples by participating in two different studies.

10. Write the questions, "How many hours do students in our school study each day? How many hours do they watch T.V?"

    Tell the students that you are going to try to get a sample from the school by using this classroom.

11. Pass out the questionnaires (see **HO1**). Explain the questionnaire to the students. Tell them that it is extremely important that each person write his/her own answers to get a sample of what each person does.

Procedure:

12. Have the students fill in the answers on the questionnaires. **Number each of the questionnaires in order of class seating** (*e.g.*, Start with row #1; have the student in the first seat of that row write #1 on the questionnaire; the second student, write #2, *etc.*).

13. Collect the questionnaires. Look at five of the questionnaires in each of the following ways:
    A. Ask for 5 volunteers who want to have their questionnaires reviewed.
    B. Select 5 from the first two-three rows.
    C. Select every 5th student in the grade book or from a roll list.
    D. Select every 5th questionnaire as it is numbered.

14. Examine the differences among the sampling procedures. Now examine all of the class questionnaires and see which of the samples most clearly represent the entire class. (Hopefully, "C"--the most random sample--will be the most representative; however, the class size is small. If none tend to represent the class, pull a larger sample and examine the differences. If all tend to represent the class, move on to a comparison with other classes in the school.)

15. Now examine the questionnaires from another class in the same grade level (if possible) or another grade level. Again compare the results. If they are similar, the students can say that their class is representative of the other class as well. If they are not similar, the students can say that their class is not representative of the other class. In this case, they will need to select a larger sample from the school if they want their questionnaire to represent the entire school.

16. Examine with the students possible areas of bias which may influence the questionnaire and how representative their sample is of the entire population: age, sex, grade, what others think may change answers written, not being truthful, wasn't serious, *etc*.

17. Review the steps in selecting a nonbiased sample (see **Resource Card 32**).

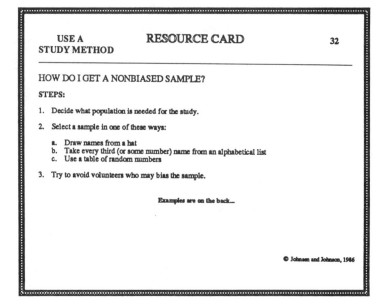

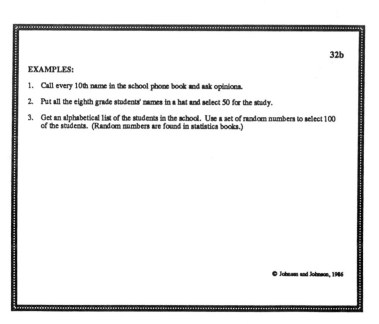

18. **ASSIGNMENT** (if desired): Pass out another set of questions about a topic. Have the students find the answers to these questions and bring the answers to class. Tell them that it is extremely important that they work by themselves. Follow the same procedure as described in this lesson. Differences among questionnaires will emphasize the importance of using more than one resource in research.

LESSON 13. DEVELOPMENT OF OBJECTIVE MEASURES

Concepts: 1. Reliability
                   2. Validity

Objective: The student will be able to develop and use objective measures in an independent study.

Materials: 1. Completed questionnaires from Lesson 12
                   2. Observation form for collecting data at home (HO2, page 116 in the Teacher's Guide)
                   3. Blank overhead or chalkboard

Evaluation: Given a topic and questions, is the student able to develop and use objective measures to collect data for an independent study?

(Note for Group Independent Study: Follow the procedure listed below with the entire group.)

Procedure:

NOTE: With younger students you may decide to select a study method for them and show them the steps as they are needed. If you do, you will omit these lessons on Study Method.

1. Explain to the students that measures they use in collecting data need to be accurate.

2. Pass out the questionnaires from Lesson 12. Have the students answer the questions again. (If the students have not filled out these questionnaires, have them answer the questions for the first time now. Then have them answer the questions again the next day before going on with this lesson).

3. When the questionnaires have been completed. Write the word "reliability" on the chalkboard. Tell them that they repeated the same procedure to see how reliable their questionnaire might be. Then write this definition next to "Reliability:" "If a measure is reliable, you will get approximately the same results each time you use it."

4. Look at the questionnaires and compare the information with the information on the ones given in Lesson 12. If the **rank order** of scores are similar, you can say that the questionnaire seems reliable with this group. If they are not similar, you can say that the questionnaire does **not** appear reliable with this group. In this case, you might ask the students why they think the scores were different.

HO1

QUESTIONNAIRE

_5_

Fill in the information below:

1. _____ Boy   _✓_ Girl
2. _Oct 2, 1976_ Birthday
3. _4_ Grade

Check only one line which is nearest to the amount of time you spend each evening watching television and doing homework:

4. The approximate amount of time I study each night:

_____ less than 30 minutes
_✓_ 30 minutes to one hour
_____ more than one hour
_____ more than two hours
_____ more than three hours

5. The approximate amount of time I watch T.V. each night:

_____ less than 30 minutes
_____ 30 minutes to one hour
_____ more than one hour
_✓_ more than two hours
_____ more than three hours
_____ I don't have a T.V.

Now complete each statement below with **one** answer:

6. My favorite subject in school is _reading_.
7. My favorite T. V. show is _The Cosby Show_.

114   © Johnson and Johnson, 1986

Procedure:

Differences may be result from attitude, motivation, memory, or the number of items. A greater number of items will produce a more reliable measurement tool.

NOTE: If the questionnaire was unreliable, you might want to develop another questionnaire with the class before going on with this lesson.

5. Tell the students that they need to have a reliable way of collecting information or data. In this way they know that the information is accurate and that differences are not related to a "bad" measure.

6. Now write the word *validity* on the chalkboard. Write this definition next to the word, *validity:* "Validity means how well the instrument measures what you want it to measure." Tell the students that one way of determining validity is to simply look at the instrument and see if it looks like it's measuring what they want it to. For example, they wouldn't use a reading test to measure math. They wouldn't ask questions about sports if they wanted to know how much they look at T.V. or study at home.

7. Ask, "Do you think this questionnaire measures what you want it to? After their responses, say to the students that they can't be sure about the validity of their questionnaires until they see if they relate to other ways that they could measure how much T.V. or much studying someone does at home.

10. Ask the students what other ways they could measure *studying* and *T.V. watching* at home. List these ideas on the chalkboard or overhead. (They might include keeping records at home, having someone else keep records at home or both.)

11. With the students, design a form that the students might use at home. List days of the week, time spent watching T.V., time spent studying, programs watched, and subjects studied (see Observation Form, HO2).

12. **ASSIGNMENT:** Have the students keep their records for one week. (You will use this data in Lesson 13).

HO2

OBSERVATION FORM

TIME	M	T	W	T	F
4:00					
4:30					
5:00					
5:30					
6:00					
6:30					
7:00					
7:30					
8:00					
8:30					
9:00					
9:30					
10:00					
10:30					
11:00					

DAYS OF WEEK

CODE: Watching T.V. =   Subject or title of T.V.
        Studying =   show is written in the
        Other activity =   box next to time and day

116   © Johnson and Johnson, 1986

LESSON 14. DATA ANALYSIS AND SUMMARY

Concepts: 1. Validity
                   2. Average (Mean)
                   3. Mode
                   4. Range
                   5. Generalization
                   6. Correlation

Objective: The student will be able to analyze, summarize and present information which is justified by the
                   study.

Materials: 1. Completed questionnaires from Teacher Guide, Lesson 12
                   2. Completed observations from Teacher Guide, Lesson 13
                   3. Blank overhead or chalkboard

Evaluation: Given a topic and questions, is the student able to analyze, summarize and present information which
                   is justified by the study?

(Note for Group Independent Study: Follow the procedure listed below with the entire group.)

Procedure:

NOTE: With younger students you may decide
to select a study method for them and
show them the steps as they are needed.
If you do, you will omit these lessons
on Study Method.

1.   List the information collected by the
     questionnaires on the chalkboard or overhead.
     Information will include the following:

QUESTIONNAIRE INFORMATION

A.   Number of boys
B.   Number of girls
C.   Average age (total months divided by #
     of students)
D.   Grade level
E.   Average time spent watching T.V.
F.   Average time spent studying
G.   Favorite subject (use number or %)
H.   Favorite T.V. show (use number or %)

NOTE: If more than one grade level or
class participated in the study, list the
responses for each class or grade level
separately.

2.   Pass out each student's questionnaire.

HO1

QUESTIONNAIRE

__/2__

Fill in the information below:

1. __✓__ Boy _____ Girl
2. __2-6-76__ Birthday
3. __4__ Grade

Check only one line which is nearest to the amount of time you spend each
evening watching television and doing homework:

4. The approximate amount of time I study each night:

    ____ less than 30 minutes
    ____ 30 minutes to one hour
    ____ more than one hour
    ____ more than two hours
    __✓__ more than three hours

5. The approximate amount of time I watch T.V. each night:

    __✓__ less than 30 minutes
    ____ 30 minutes to one hour
    ____ more than one hour
    ____ more than two hours
    ____ more than three hours
    ____ I don't have a T.V.

Now complete each statement below with one answer:

6. My favorite subject in school is __Math__
7. My favorite T. V. show is __3-2-1 Contact__

114   © Johnson and Johnson, 1986

Procedure:

3. Have students look at data that they collected at home. Have them list problems that they might have had in collecting the data. Write these on the chalkboard or overhead. (They might have had difficulty remembering; had an unusual week; not been allowed to watch T.V.; stayed up later than the observation form allowed, *etc*.). Tell them that this information will have an effect on the data collected and will be reported with the results of the study.

4. Have each student figure the average number of hours that they studied during the week (*i.e.*, add total number of hours and divide by 5) and the average number of hours that they watched T.V. (*i.e.*, add total number of hours and divide by 5). Have them indicate whether or not they watched their "favorite show." If time allows, have the students determine the average amount of time that they studied each subject.

5. List the information collected by observation next to the questionnaire information on the chalkboard or overhead:

   OBSERVATION INFORMATION

   A. Number of boys
   B. Number of girls
   C. Average age
   D. Grade level
   E. Average time spent watching T.V.
   F. Average time spent studying
   G. Average time spent studying each subject (take averages for each subject and divide by the number of students in the class)
   H. Watched favorite T.V. show (use number or per cent)

   NOTE: If more than one grade level or class participated in the study, list the responses for each class or grade level separately.

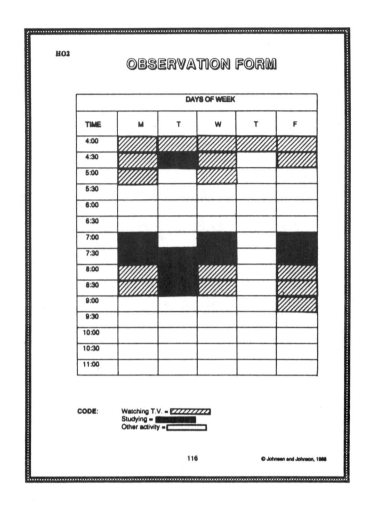

Procedure:

6. Compare the questionnaire with the observation form. If the two are similar, you can say that the questionnaire **appears** to measure validly T.V. and Study times. (However, the questionnaire might have influenced how the students collected data at home.) If the two forms are not alike, the students might consider one or more of the following reasons for this difference:

    A. The questionnaire was not valid (didn't measure what it was supposed to).

    B. Data collected on the observation form was not reliable. Students forgot to collect data or indicate times, didn't want to collect data, *etc*.

    C. Data was collected over an entire week instead of just one time.

    D. The observation form was difficult to use.

    NOTE: If the data from the two measures are not alike, you may want to do *one* of the following:
    1. Change the observation form.
    2. Repeat the collection of data.
    3. Add an additional observer at home to improve the relationship between the two measures.
    4. Exclude the questionnaire from the rest of this lesson as an invalid measure.
    5. Accept the inadequacy of the current measure and go to Step 7.

7. Now place these **generalizations** on the chalkboard (with the data from your study):

    A. On the average students in (name of state) watch __hours of T.V. each week. On the average students in (name of state) study __hours at home each week.

    B. On the average students in (name of city or town) watch __hours of T.V. each week. On the average students in (name of city or town) study __hours at home each week.

... to take a step into the future we need to shift our weight to the opposite foot

w.i. thompson

Procedure:

    C. On the average students in (name of school) watch __hours of T.V. each week. On the average students in (name of school) study __hours at home each week.

    D. On the average students in (grade level) watch __hours of T.V. each week. On the average students in (grade level) study __hours at home each week.

    E. On the average students in (name of class) watch ___hours of T.V. each week. On the average students in (name of class) study ___ hours at home each week.

8. Ask the students, "What **generalization** can we make from the results of our study?" Unless you involved more students in your school, the only statement that can be made from the study is "E."

9. Ask the students what further analyses may be made with the data. You may suggest the following:

    A. Figuring differences between boys and girls

    B. Figuring the **mode** (the **greatest number** of hours spent watching T.V. and/or studying; the greatest number of hours spent on each subject, etc.)

    C. Figuring the **range** (the least **and the** greatest number of hours spent watching T.V. and/or studying; the least and the greatest number of hours spent on each subject, etc.).

    D. Figuring the relationship between T.V. and study times. To do this **correlation**, follow these steps:

        (1) Make or get graph paper.

        (2) Along the horizontal line or X axis, mark the number of thirty-minute intervals of Study Time.

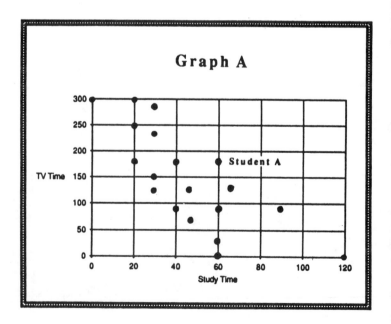

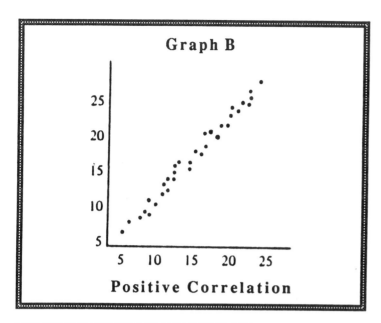

Graph B

Positive Correlation

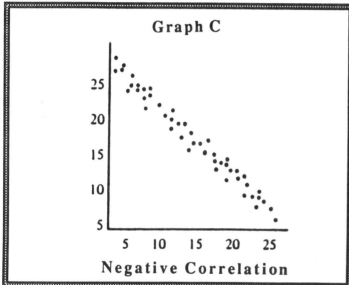

Graph C

Negative Correlation

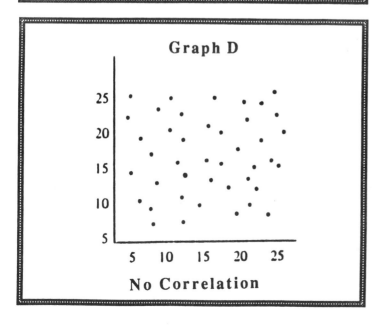

Graph D

No Correlation

Procedure:

(3) Along the vertical line or Y axis, mark the number of thirty-minute intervals of T.V. Time.

(4) Plot the sets of data for each student. For example, Student *A* studied an average of **one** hour each day and watched an average of **two and one half hours** of T.V. each day (see Graph A). When all of the sets of data are plotted, look at the graph to determine the relationship (see Graphs B, C, D). (Graph A shows that there is a somewhat negative relationship between watching T.V. and study time--the more T.V. watched, the less study time.)

NOTE: If you are interested in computing actual statistics for correlations, reliability, validity, *etc.*, consult an elementary statistics book or use *Handbook in Research and Evaluation* by Stephen Isaac and William Michael, EdITS publishers, San Diego, California 92107. This book is an excellent resource for persons who do not have a background in statistics and/or research.

10. Summarize the lesson by reviewing the following principles:

A. When you study a topic, you want to make sure that you have reliable and valid measures.

B. Reliability means that you will get approximately the same results every time you use it.

C. Validity means that the instrument measures what it's supposed to measure.

D. You want to make sure that you get a nonbiased sample from the total population. You will want to use a variety of resources. You will want to use a random sample unless you have one particular group that you are using...only one class.

Procedure:

    E. You will want to only make generalizations that can be justified by your study.

    F. Further analysis of your information can be made by looking at averages, modes, correlations, and ranges.

11. **ASSIGNMENT**: Have each of the students look at their questions and identify the following:

    A. Measures that they will use to examine each question in their study

    B. How they will identify the reliability and validity of their measures

    C. How they will select their population

    D. How they plan to analyze their data

There is a tide in the affairs of men which, taken at the flood, leads on to fortune; omitted, all the voyage of their life is bound in shallows and in miseries. We must take the current while it serves or lose our ventures.

Shakespeare

LESSON 15. COLLECT INFORMATION

Concept: Collect Information

Objective: Students will examine various ways to collect information about a topic.

Materials: 1. Resource Card 33
                2. Student Booklet, pages 2 and 15

Evaluation: Given a topic to study, the student will be able to select three ways that they will collect information.

(Note for Group Independent Study: If you would like the students to work together as a group, decide on the resources and processes that they will be using and teach these to the entire group.)

Procedure:

1. Have the students look in the **Student Booklets, page 15** and at **Resource Card 33.** Have the students talk about the various ways to collect information about a topic. Have them list these in their student booklets. (If the students rely on the encyclopedia, explain that it will give them a good, brief overview, but they will want to use more and different kinds of resources.)

2. Select one process for collecting information that most students will be using, such as *note taking* or *brainstorming*, and teach it as a group lesson. (The processes are listed on **Resource Card 33.**)

3. After they have learned this process, divide students into small groups according to the other processes that they will use such as surveying or interviewing. (Not all students will use the same methods of gathering information.) Teach the skills as needed to each small group.

NOTE: You may decide to teach only one process to the students for their first independent study. To teach a specific process:
   A. Tell students the name of the process that they will use.
   B. Tell them the definition of the process.
   C. Show examples (how to do it).
   D. Show nonexamples (how *not* to do it).
   E. Model the process.
   F. Give them a copy of the steps or have them look at Resource Cards.
   G. Have them try each step by practicing or role playing.

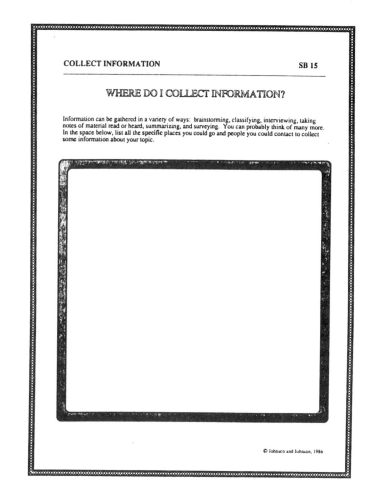

COLLECT INFORMATION   SB 15

WHERE DO I COLLECT INFORMATION?

Information can be gathered in a variety of ways: brainstorming, classifying, interviewing, taking notes of material read or heard, summarizing, and surveying. You can probably think of many more. In the space below, list all the specific places you could go and people you could contact to collect some information about your topic.

© Johnson and Johnson, 1986

Procedure:

5. When students have been introduced to a process, allow them enough time to collect the information needed. Provide structure by giving them a deadline to complete their information gathering!

6. **ASSIGNMENT:** Have students check the three ways that they will collect information in the **Student Booklets, page 2.**

COLLECT INFORMATION	**RESOURCE CARD**	33

INDEX

WAYS WE GATHER AND ORGANIZE INFORMATION	CARDS
Brainstorm	34 - 35
Classify	36
Interview	37 - 40
Summarize	41 - 48
Survey	49 - 55
Take Notes	56 - 60
Write Letters	61 - 62

© Johnson and Johnson, 1986

Some books are to be tasted, others to be swallowed, and some few to be chewed and digested.

F. BACON

LESSON 16. COLLECT INFORMATION: BRAINSTORM

Concepts:
1. Brainstorm
2. Fluency
3. Flexibility
4. Elaboration
5. Originality

Objective: Given a stimulus, the students will use the process of brainstorming to develop a list of at least 20 varied responses.

Materials:
1. Resource Card 34, 35
2. Teacher Guide, Lesson 7, page 16
3. Large sheets of butcher paper (1 sheet for each group of 4 or 5)
4. Felt markers
5. Blank overhead or chalkboard

Evaluation: Given a stimulus, did the students use the process of brainstorming in developing a list of at least 20 varied responses?

Procedure:

1. Explain the purpose of brainstorming: It helps us think of many, varied ideas related to a topic. This technique is used by many scientists, advertisers, writers, artists, and business persons to stimulate creative and critical thinking.

2. State the rules of brainstorming or post them (see **Resource Card 34**). (You might even have students make posters of them.)

   A. Think of many, varied ideas.
   B. Do not judge ideas while they are being given.
   C. Combine ideas and use everyone's ideas.
   D. Accept all ideas, no matter how wild they may seem.

3. Explain each rule and give an example.

4. Select a topic that everyone knows, choose several students and take them through the brainstorming process for three minutes. Write their ideas on the chalkboard. Point out how the brainstorming rules were followed (or not followed). Select another topic that everyone knows and repeat the process. This time have *the students* point out the brainstorming rules that were followed (or not followed). Continue in this way until the rules appear to be understood.

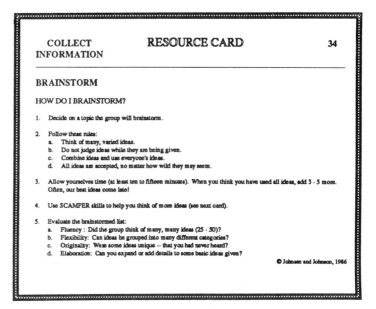

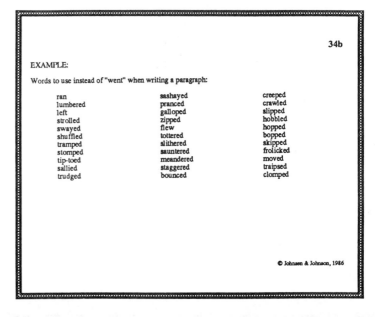

Procedure:

5.   With the group, decide on a topic to brainstorm.

NOTE: For a large group session:

A.   Use the overhead projector or chalkboard.
B.   State the topic and allow students one or two minutes of silent thinking.
C.   Record all responses given as quickly as possible.
D.   When the students seem to have exhausted all ideas, wait. Encourage them to think of 3 - 5 more ideas. Frequently best responses come late!

For small group sessions:

A.   Divide the class into groups of three to five students.
B.   Give each group a large sheet of butcher paper and markers. Have the group choose either one recorder (they may want to take turns, since it's difficult for the recorder to contribute ideas) or have all students write their own ideas as they say them aloud.
C.   State the topic. Tell them to think of at least 20 different responses.
D.   Have each group generate responses.
E.   As groups are brainstorming, circulate around the room and make sure that the students are following rules. Encourage them to record all ideas and to defer judgment!   They may need guidance for the first few sessions.

6.   You may wish to help students think of more ideas by teaching them another type of brainstorming technique which is called "SCAMPERing" (see **Resource Card** 35). SCAMPER is an an acronym for:

COLLECT INFORMATION	RESOURCE CARD	35

BRAINSTORM		SCAMPER SKILLS
S	Substitute	Who or what else instead? Other ingredient, material, place?
C	Combine	Put several things together, blend, assemble?
A	Adapt	What else is like this? What could I copy and change?
M	Modify Magnify	Change the meaning, add to it, give it a new twist? Make it bigger, longer, taller, deeper?
P	Put to other uses	Use in other places? Use it in a new and different way? Change it to use in a new way?
E	Eliminate	Take something away; make it smaller, lower, shorter?
R	Rearrange Reverse	Make another pattern, another sequence? What is the opposite, turn it around?

© Johnsen and Johnson, 1986

Procedure:

S   Substitute
Who or what else instead?   Other ingredient, material, place?

C   Combine
Put several things together, blend.

A   Adapt
What else is like it? How could it be changed?

M   Modify Magnify
Change the meaning, add to it, give it a new twist?   Make it bigger, longer, taller?

P   Put to other uses
Use in other places, use in new way?

E   Eliminate
Take something away, make it smaller, lower, shorter?

R   Rearrange Reverse?
Make another pattern, another sequence?   What is the opposite, turn it around?

9. Have students try one or more of the SCAMPER exercises on an idea. (For help in using the exercises, see **Teacher Guide, Lesson 7, page 16.**)

10. Help the students evaluate their list.

A. Fluency: Did the group think of many, many ideas? (25 - 50?)
B. Flexibility: Can ideas be grouped into many different categories?
C. Originality: Were some ideas unique to the group?
D. Elaboration: Can students expand or add details to some basic ideas given? can they add who, what, when, where, why and how?

11. **ASSIGNMENT:** Have the students use the brainstorming process to collect information on their topics.

the function
of intelligence
is not to copy
but to invent.
*** J.h.Rush

LESSON 17.   COLLECT INFORMATION: CLASSIFY

Concepts: 1. Classify
                   2. Categorize

Objective: Students will classify sets of items by organizing them into groups with one or more characteristics.

Materials: 1. Resource Card 36
                   2. Blank overhead an/or chalkboard

Evaluation: Given sets of items, did the students organize them into groups with one or more characteristics?

Procedure:

1. Explain that the purpose of classifying information is to help organize and categorize information in an understandable way. To classify means to organize items into groups that are alike in some way. Items may be objects, words, thoughts, ideas, hypotheses, problems, *etc.*

2. Show them some items that are classified:

    A. By one characteristic
    B. By two characteristics
    C. By characteristics that are observable
    D. By characteristics that are inferred
    E. By characteristics that change as the examples change (*e.g.*, big, fat, tall, *etc.*)
    F. By characteristics that are "either, or" (*e.g.*, an out is made by three strikes, a caught fly, a forced out, or touching a person with the ball)

3. Select, or have the students select, a set of items to classify (*e.g.*, musical instruments, automobiles, TV shows, songs, furniture, books, *etc.*). Write these on the board (see **Resource Card 36** for an example).

4. Have the students think of all the various ways the items are alike (*e.g.*, color, size, function, type).

5. Encourage the students to decide on a few headings that describe the characteristics of the items. Write a few headings across the board and divide by drawing vertical lines between each of them. You may include a column for items that the students might suggest that do not fit into any of the categories (*i.e.*, nonexamples).

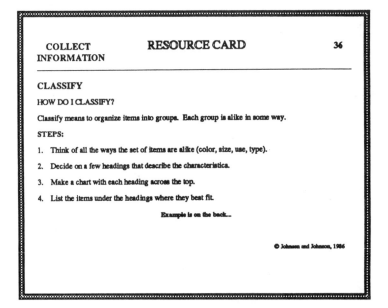

COLLECT
INFORMATION   **RESOURCE CARD**   **36**

CLASSIFY

HOW DO I CLASSIFY?

Classify means to organize items into groups. Each group is alike in some way.

STEPS:

1. Think of all the ways the set of items are alike (color, size, use, type).

2. Decide on a few headings that describe the characteristics.

3. Make a chart with each heading across the top.

4. List the items under the headings where they best fit.

Example is on the back...

© Johnson and Johnson, 1986

36b

CLASSIFY

EXAMPLE:

drums, violin, guitar, flute, trumpet, piano, bongo, symbol, clarinet, tamborine, banjo, trombone, harp

Classify the set of examples:

1. Think of ways the above items are alike: musical instruments, percussion, stringed, wind.
2. Decide on appropriate headings: percussion, stringed, wind instruments.
3. Make a chart to show the categories.
4. List each item under the appropriate heading.

MUSICAL INSTRUMENTS

Percussion	Stringed	Wind
drum	violin	flute
bongo	guitar	trumpet
symbol	banjo	clarinet
piano	harp	trombone
tambori		

© Johnson and Johnson, 1986

Procedure:

6. Have the students write the items under the appropriate headings. If a suggested item is not an example of what students are classifying, place it in the "non-example" column.

7. Have the students repeat steps five and six, using a different set of headings.

8. Ask the students what they observed about classifying:

   A. Students may observe that the more similar the characteristics are, the more difficult they are to classify.

   B. Students may observe that items may be classified in many different ways.

   C. Students may observe that similar items that are "nonexamples" help to clarify the "examples."

   D. Students may observe that the headings may change as the items that need to be classified change.

9. ASSIGNMENT: Have the students use this process in organizing their topics. For example, they might take their note cards and sort them into similar groups; they might examine all of the definitions of their topics and see if there are some common characteristics; they might create a new classification system for some aspect of their topic. If necessary, have them brainstorm various ways that they might use the classification process in their independent studies.

LESSON 18.   COLLECT INFORMATION: INTERVIEW

Concept: Interview

Objective: Students will generate a list of interview questions and practice questioning strategies
                  through role playing.

Materials: 1. Any published interviews from magazines
                  2. Resource Cards 37, 38, 39, 40
                  3. Blank overhead or chalkboard

Evaluation: Given a role-play situation, did the students generate a list of interview questions and practice
                  questioning strategies?

Procedure:

1. Explain the purpose of an interview: to obtain information directly from a person who answers questions. Interviewing is an excellent way of collecting information that cannot be easily found in books or magazines. It also can provide students with personal perspectives about their topics (see **Resource Card 37** for additional reasons).

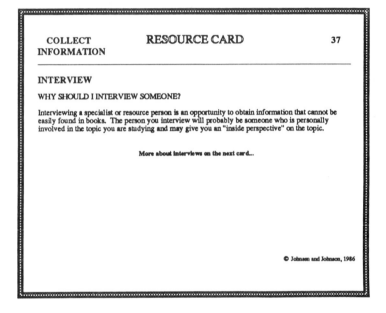

2. Write the steps on the overhead or chalkboard to be used *before* an interview (see **Resource Card 38**):

    • Select a person who knows about the subject you are studying.

    • Call or write the person to set up an interview. Always state name, who you are, what you are studying, and why you want to interview the person.

    • Make an appointment for a specific day, time, and place. Let the person know approximately how much time it will take (not over 30 minutes!). Try to be flexible and work around the interviewee's schedule.

    • Do your homework on the person. Know something about the person, why he/she might be helpful to you, and read anything he/she may have written.

    • Make notes to take into the interview: full name of the interviewee; date, time and place of interview; background information about the person.

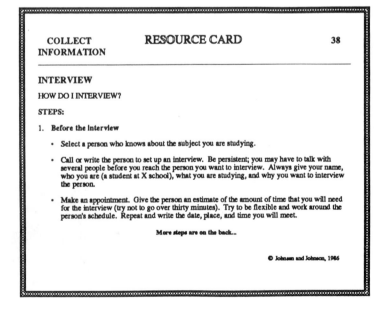

38b

INTERVIEW

STEPS (continued):

- Do your homework; know who the person is, why he/she might be helpful to you, and learn something about the interviewee before the interview.

- Make some notes to take into the interview: name of person being interviewed, date and time of interview, position or occupation of person, why this person was selected, the topic that will be discussed, background information on the person.

- Write a list of questions you would like to ask the person.

More steps are on the next card...

© Johnson and Johnson, 1986

COLLECT INFORMATION   RESOURCE CARD   39

INTERVIEW

STEPS (continued):

2. **During the interview**

- When you meet the person, introduce yourself, shake hands and thank him/her for giving you the interview.

- If you wish to tape record the interview, ask the person for permission.

- Ask the questions from the list, but don't limit yourself to the list. If the person is talking about something of interest, ask follow-up questions. Much of our most interesting information comes from spontaneous communication.

- Be a good listener; look directly at the person.

- Listen for clue words and phrases that tell you something important is coming.

More steps are on the back...

© Johnson and Johnson, 1986

39b

INTERVIEW

STEPS (continued):

- Take a few notes about important information.

- Allow a few seconds of silent time after the person stops talking. Allow time for the person to think through responses and perhaps add more information.

- Try to visualize or see pictures in your mind.

- Keep to the time limit. If you have told the person that the interview would be no more that thirty minutes, be sure to stop after thirty minutes. If they want to spend more time, they can tell you.

- When the interview is finished, thank the person again and express that he/she has been very helpful to you in your study.

More steps are on the next card...

© Johnson and Johnson, 1986

Procedure:

- Write a list of questions you would like to ask the person.

3. Pretend that you are calling a person to interview. Have the students observe what you do. Model how to do it correctly. Let the students explain what you did correctly. Model how to do it incorrectly. Let the students explain what you forgot to do or what you did incorrectly.

4. Now list the steps for what to do *during* an interview (see **Resource Card 39**).

   - Introduce yourself, shake hands, and thank him/her for giving you the interview.

   - If you wish to tape record the interview, ask the person for permission.

   - Ask questions from the list, but don't limit yourself to that list.

   - Be a good listener. Look directly at the person.

   - Listen for words and phrases that tell you something important is coming.

   - Take a few notes about important information.

   - Allow a few second of silent time after the person stops talking.

   - Try to visualize what the person is saying.

   - Keep to your time limit.

   - Thank the person again when the interview is finished.

5. Select a student to interview as a model for the class. Ask the student what might be an area of interest that he/she would like to discuss in an interview (or have a topic in mind and select the student accordingly).

Procedure:

6. Have the rest of the class generate a list of questions that could be asked to obtain specific information about the topic. (See "Ask Questions" section and guide students to use *most thinking* questions in the interview.) Guide their questioning to allow the interviewee to expand on an idea rather than answer with one-word replies. This is the brainstorming part of the interviewing process and students should be encouraged to think of many, many questions (without judgment). Later, evaluate and select the best few questions to use.

7. Look over the list of questions and have the students combine similar questions, mark the questions that ask most thinking questions, cross out questions that require a "yes" or "no" response. Select the most appropriate 8 - 10 questions.

8. Sequence the questions with students in the order in which they will be asked. On a piece of paper or index cards, write the questions in order and leave blank spaces where the answers will be written.

9. Seat the student to be interviewed in front of the class with a chair for the teacher. If appropriate, go over some of the pre-interview preparations aloud with the class using the student and the present situation.

10. Role play the simulated interview with the student. For later evaluation have each student observe a different step that should be used during the interview.

11. After the interview, have the class evaluate the interview using the steps listed on **Resource Card 39**.

12. List the following steps on the chalkboard or overhead (see **Resource Card 40**):

    • Review your notes as soon as possible.

    • Write the interview in paragraph form.

    • Write a thank you note.

COLLECT INFORMATION	RESOURCE CARD	40

INTERVIEW

STEPS (continued):

3. After the Interview

• Review the notes and tape recording as soon as possible while the information is fresh on your mind.

• Write the interview in paragraph form to include in the report.

• Write the interviewed person a thank you note telling how much you appreciate the time that was spent helping you with the research project.

• If possible, send the person a copy of the report you write or invite him/her to view the product when you present it to the class.

© Johnson and Johnson, 1986

Procedure:

- Send the person a final copy of your product and/or invite him/her to your presentation.

13. Again, model these final steps with the students. Do it correctly and then incorrectly. Have the students evaluate each time, telling what was done correctly and what was done incorrectly.

14. You may want to invite an adult from the school to be interviewed for more practice or you may want to divide the class into pairs and have each pair interview one another.

15. **ASSIGNMENT:** Have the students select someone to interview, following the steps listed on **Resource Cards 39-40**. You might wish to review the students' sets of questions prior to their interviews.

It is the supreme art
of the teacher
to awaken joy
in creative expression
and knowledge

A. Einstein

LESSON 19: COLLECT INFORMATION: SUMMARIZE

Concept: Summarize

Objective: Students will read a passage, categorize the type of information given, then sort the relevant information.

Materials: 1. Story from textbook, magazine or newspaper article
                     2. Resource Cards 41-48
                     3. Teacher Guide, Lesson 17
                     4. Information about student topics
                     5. Blank overhead or chalkboard

Evaluation: Given a passage, did the students categorize the type of information given and sort the relevant information?

Procedure:

1. Explain the purpose of summarizing: to sort through a large amount of information and put the main ideas into a shortened form that can be easily understood.

2. Discuss how to summarize information (see **Resource Card 41**).

    •   Look over the material you are studying.

    •   Sort the information into categories, such as facts, opinions, causes, effects, problems, solutions, main ideas, parts.

    •   Categories can be found by locating information that tells how things are similar or different (see **Teacher Guide, Lesson 17** on classifying for more information).

    •   Write the categories on paper or note cards.

    •   Write notes from the material under the **appropriate category heading.**

COLLECT INFORMATION | **RESOURCE CARD** | 41

SUMMARIZE

HOW DO I SUMMARIZE?

To summarize means to sort through a large amount of information and put the main ideas into a shortened form that others can understand.

STEPS:

1. Look at the notes or material you are studying.

2. Sort the information into categories such as facts, opinions, causes, effects, problems, solutions, main ideas, parts.

5. Label the categories.

6. Decide the best way to present the information, then put the information into that form.

More about summarizing on the next card...

© Johnsen and Johnson, 1986

COLLECT INFORMATION | **RESOURCE CARD** | 42

SUMMARIZE

WAYS TO SUMMARIZE INFORMATION

1. Identify examples and/or facts, then make a generalization or statement about them (see Resource Card 43 for example).

2. Describe the parts (see Resource Card 44 for example).

3. Identify causes and effects (see Resource Card 45 for example).

4. Make comparisons (see Resource Card 46 for example).

5. Show a sequence (see Resource Card 47 for example).

6. Identify problems and solutions (see Resource Card 48 for example).

Example is on the next card...

© Johnsen & Johnson, 1986

| COLLECT INFORMATION | RESOURCE CARD | 43 |

SUMMARIZE

EXAMPLE:

1. Identify facts, then make a generalization or statement about them, or make a generalization and support it with facts.

   Facts: After the Civil War, the South's economy collapsed.
   The southern states had no government.
   Plantation owners had no or few former slaves to farm the tobacco and cotton crops.
   Thousands of slaves had no skills to work outside the plantation.

   Generalization: The South was hurt by the Civil War.

   Another example is on the next card...

   © Johnsen & Johnson, 1986

| COLLECT INFORMATION | RESOURCE CARD | 44 |

SUMMARIZE

EXAMPLE:

2. Describe the parts.

   • Describe the major battles of the Civil War (location, generals, victors, *etc.*).

Fort Sumpter, SC	Appomattox, VA
Bull Run, PA	Fredericksburg, VA
Gettysburg, PA	Perryville, KY
Vicksburg, MI	

   • Discuss information about generals of the war.

Ulysses S. Grant	William T. Sherman
Robert E. Lee	Joseph E. Johnston
George B. McClellan	"Stonewall" Jackson

   Another example is on the next card...

   © Johnsen and Johnson, 1986

| COLLECT INFORMATION | RESOURCE CARD | 45 |

SUMMARIZE

EXAMPLE:

3. Identify causes and effects.

Causes of the Civil War	Effects of the Civil War
slavery issue	South's economy collapsed
The Missouri Compromise	Southern states without government
Dred Scott Case	Slaves were free but knew few trades
states' rights	
secession	

   Another example is on the next card...

   © Johnsen & Johnson, 1986

Procedure:

3. List the different ways to summarize information from **Resource Card 42** on the overhead or chalkboard. (Depending on the level of the students, you may choose one basic way of summarizing or you may list all of the methods.)

   • Identify examples, then make a generalization.

   • Describe the parts.

   • Identify causes and effects.

   • Make comparisons.

   • Show a sequence.

   • Identify problems and solutions.

4. Now take some information familiar to the students and show them how to summarize it in the various ways listed above. (You might want to use the examples listed on **Resource Cards 43-48**.)

5. If needed, repeat the process with more information until all of the students understand how to summarize using each method.

6. Now select one method. Write it on the overhead or chalkboard.

7. Divide the students into small groups. Have the students read a passage in a textbook, an article from a magazine and/or an item from the newspaper. Have each small group summarize the information using the method listed.

8. Now have each small group tell how they summarized the information. Have the students identify the best way(s) that the information was summarized and have them explain why.

9. Repeat this process with the same method or a different method until the students appear to understand how to summarize, using each of the methods. (See the next page for an assignment.)

Procedure:

10. **ASSIGNMENT.** Have the students summarize some information that they may have collected about their topics. Allow them to use any of the methods that have been presented.

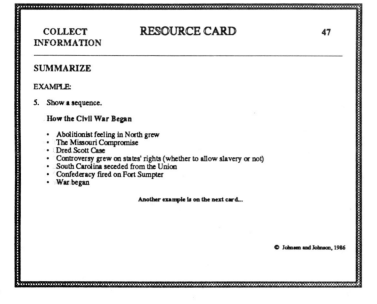

COLLECT INFORMATION   **RESOURCE CARD**   46

SUMMARIZE

EXAMPLE:

4. Make comparisons.

North	South
• against slavery	• for slavery
• industrial economy	• farm economy

Another example is on the next card...

© Johnson and Johnson, 1986

COLLECT INFORMATION   **RESOURCE CARD**   48

SUMMARIZE

EXAMPLE:

6. Identify problems and solutions.

Possible Problems

- Few slaves could read or write
- Slaves knew few trades
- Hard feelings between people of North and South
- Families split by war (some members fought with North and some fought with South)

Solutions

- Select one problem and study what was done to alleviate the problem
- Add your opinions and ideas about how the problem might have been remedied.

© Johnson and Johnson, 1986

COLLECT INFORMATION   **RESOURCE CARD**   47

SUMMARIZE

EXAMPLE:

5. Show a sequence.

How the Civil War Began

- Abolitionist feeling in North grew
- The Missouri Compromise
- Dred Scott Case
- Controversy grew on states' rights (whether to allow slavery or not)
- South Carolina seceded from the Union
- Confederacy fired on Fort Sumpter
- War began

Another example is on the next card...

© Johnson and Johnson, 1986

LESSON 20: COLLECT INFORMATION: SURVEY

Concept: Survey

Objective: Students will conduct a simulated survey, analyze and report the results.

Materials: 1. Examples of survey results from magazines
                  2. Examples of questionnaires from restaurants
                  3. Resource Cards 49, 50, 51, 52, 53, 54, 55
                  4. Teacher's Guide, Lessons 12 and 14

Evaluation: Given a simulated situation, were the students able to conduct a survey, analyze and report the results?

Procedure:

1. Explain the purpose of surveying: to examine what a group of people think about something. A survey provides us with a system to gather, process and analyze information (see Resource Card 49).

2. Tell students that surveys may be conducted in several ways:

    • **face-to-face interview**

    The surveyor interviews individuals in person and records their responses.

    • **telephone interview**

    The surveyor asks individuals questions by telephone and records all responses.

    • **questionnaire**

    The surveyor mails or gives a set of questions to persons; the persons record their responses to the questions; the persons return their responses to the surveyor.

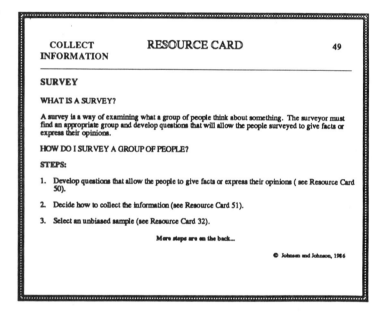

COLLECT INFORMATION   RESOURCE CARD   49

SURVEY

WHAT IS A SURVEY?

A survey is a way of examining what a group of people think about something. The surveyor must find an appropriate group and develop questions that will allow the people surveyed to give facts or express their opinions.

HOW DO I SURVEY A GROUP OF PEOPLE?

STEPS:

1. Develop questions that allow the people to give facts or express their opinions (see Resource Card 50).

2. Decide how to collect the information (see Resource Card 51).

3. Select an unbiased sample (see Resource Card 32).

More steps are on the back...

© Johnson and Johnson, 1986

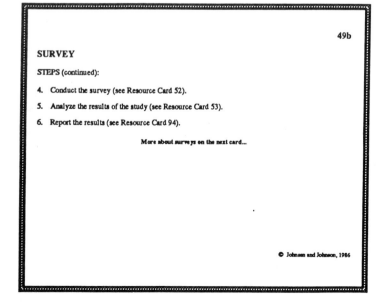

49b

SURVEY

STEPS (continued):

4. Conduct the survey (see Resource Card 52).

5. Analyze the results of the study (see Resource Card 53).

6. Report the results (see Resource Card 94).

More about surveys on the next card...

© Johnson and Johnson, 1986

Procedure:

3. Ask the class for examples of each kind of survey.

    •   **face-to-face interviews**

        This kind is used frequently on television, on radio and in magazines and newspapers, *i.e.* T.V. news gives us a sample of how a segment of the public is thinking about certain issues.

    •   **telephone interviews**

        This type is used in business and in politics to find out what kind of products people use or who their preferred candidate might be.

    •   **questionnaires**

        This type is used by business and industry to obtain opinions about products or ideas, *i.e.* some fast food restaurants use cards to judge the quality of food, service and appearance.

4. Show some examples of questionnaires from magazines or restaurants.

5. Discuss what the questionnaires have in common and how they are different. For example:

    •   What kind of background information is requested?

        Information requested will vary according to what the survey is trying to find out. Age, occupation, sex, school, grade, city, state, ethnicity or religion may be included; however, the students may note that the respondent's name is often omitted to ensure anonymity.

    •   What kind of format is used?

        Formats may require a simple yes/no; a three-point scale such as "Extremely Satisfied," "Somewhat Satisfied," "Never Satisfied;" a four-point scale such as "Yearly," "Monthly," "Weekly," "Never," *etc.*

COLLECT
INFORMATION   **RESOURCE CARD**   54

SURVEY

EXAMPLE:

1. I wanted to do a survey in my school about pets.

    •   How many students in my school own pets?
    •   What kinds of pets do they have?
    •   How many pets do they have?
    •   Which grade has more pets?
    •   Do more boys or girls own pets?

2. Since it would be too difficult and too costly to survey *all* students in the school, I selected two grades as the sample.

3. I decided to distribute the questionnaire to all 5th and 7th grade teachers and ask them to have their classes complete the survey within the next week.

4. I picked up the completed questionnaires from the teachers after one week. I knew that it would be impossible to have all the questionnaires returned, but I received about 70% back.

More steps are on the back...

© Johnsen and Johnson, 1986

54b

SURVEY

EXAMPLE (continued):

5. I looked back at the questions I had asked at the beginning of the survey.

6. I talleyed the information from the questionnaires in several ways:

    •   number and kind of pets fifth graders reported
    •   number and kind of pets seventh graders reported
    •   number and kind of pets reported in all
    •   number and kind of pets males reported
    •   number and kind of pets females reported

7. I wrote an answer to each of the five questions asked and decided that the best way to show the results was by using a graph.

8. I thought about other questions and wondered if the results would have been different in a school from a different part of the country. I wondered if my friend from another state would like to do the same survey, and we could compare the results.

More about surveys on the next card...

© Johnsen and Johnson, 1986

COLLECT
INFORMATION   **RESOURCE CARD**   55

SURVEY

                              PET SURVEY

Grade Level _____   Sex _____

How many pets do you have? Write the number on the line.

_____ dogs
_____ cats
_____ turtles
_____ fish
_____ horses
_____ birds
_____ other _____

Graph of results is on the back...

© Johnsen and Johnson, 1986

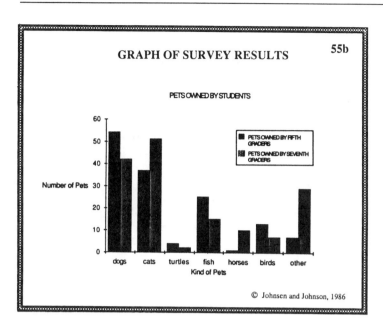

GRAPH OF SURVEY RESULTS 55b

PETS OWNED BY STUDENTS

© Johnsen and Johnson, 1986

COLLECT
INFORMATION

RESOURCE CARD 50

SURVEY

DEVELOP QUESTIONS THAT GIVE FACTS OR ALLOW PEOPLE TO EXPRESS THEIR OPINIONS.

STEPS:

1. Background Information

   Background information tells you about the people who are completing the survey. This information on a person can be as important to your survey as the person's opinions.

   Possible Background Information:*

   Name _____ Age_____ Sex _____
   Occupation _____ Ethnicity _____
   School _____ Grade _____
   City _____ State _____

   * Decide which information is important to your survey. You may not need to use all of the items on Background Information.

   Questions are on the back...

   © Johnsen and Johnson, 1986

50b

SURVEY

2. Ways to formulate questions

   Open-ended Format

   How do you feel about the food in the school cafeteria? _____

   Choice Format   Yes   No

   Do you like the food in the school cafeteria?   ____   ____

   Rating Scale   Extremely   Somewhat   Not Very
                             Delicious   Delicious Delicious

   How do you rate the food in the school cafeteria? ____   ____   ____

                       Always Frequently Sometimes Never

   How often do you eat in the school cafeteria? ____   ____   ____   ____

   © Johnsen and Johnson, 1986

Procedure:

6. Discuss the steps involved in conducting a survey (see **Resource Card 49**).

   - Decide on the information you want to know.

   - Decide how the survey will be conducted, *i.e.*, face-to-face or telephone interview, or questionnaire.

   - Select an unbiased sample.

   - Conduct the survey and collect the information. Tally the results.

   - Analyze the information.

   - Report the results in some way.

7. Tell the students that in learning how to conduct a survey, they will participate in a survey themselves (see **Resource Card 54 and 55** for an example survey).

8. Have the students think of something that they would like to know about the class. Consider some of the following:

   - Students born in what month have the most height?

   - Students born in which half of the school year have the most siblings?

   - Do more boys or girls play musical instruments?

   - Do boys or girls have more pets?

   - How much time is spent talking on the telephone each night? watching T.V.? doing homework?

9. Have the students generate questions that relate to what they want to know about the class. Be sure to include any demographic information that is needed (see **Resource Card 50**).

10. Have the students evaluate the questions by seeing if they relate to the purpose of the survey and if the words are clear and unambiguous.

Procedure:

11. Decide on the format that will be used (see **Resource Card 50**).

12. With the students prepare the questionnaire by writing it on the chalkboard. Let everyone make copies of the questionnaire.

13. Decide how to collect the information (see **Resource Card 51**). For example, each student may answer the questions and then turn them in for the tally or survey one another in a face-to-face interview.

14. Conduct the survey (see **Resource Card 52**).

15. Help them analyze the results (see **Resource Card 53** and **Teacher Guide, Lesson 14, pages 40-45** for ways to analyze data). They should look back at the original questions and make sure that their data answer them.

16. Either model the reporting of the results or have various class members report the results (see **Resource Cards 78-83** on graphs, if needed).

NOTE: For any students who have had experience with surveys, teach them how to obtain an unbiased sample:

Since it is not always possible to obtain everyone's ideas from a survey form, students must figure out a way to get the most representative sample from a population. In helping them select an nonbiased sample, follow the procedure listed in the **Teacher's Guide, Lesson 12, pages 35-37** with the questionnaire that the students developed.

17. **ASSIGNMENT:** Have the students develop their own survey forms to collect information about their topics.

COLLECT INFORMATION **RESOURCE CARD** **51**

SURVEY

DECIDE HOW TO COLLECT THE INFORMATION

The answers to the survey questions may be obtained in several ways, such as:

1. in person

2. by telephone

3. through written format

- mail, or
- distributed as a handout

More about surveys on the next card...

© Johnsen and Johnson, 1986

COLLECT INFORMATION **RESOURCE CARD** **52**

SURVEY

CONDUCT THE SURVEY

STEPS:

1. Make copies of the questionnaire for each person who will be surveyed (use one questionnaire per person).

2. Ask the questions to the selected group of people. If you distribute or mail the questionnaire, include written directions to tell people what to do and how to return the information to you.

3. It is practically impossible to have all questionnaires returned. However, the more that are returned, the better the survey will be.

4. When the questionnaires are returned, you may begin to analyze the results (see next Resource Card).

More about surveys on the next card...

© Johnsen and Johnson, 1986

COLLECT INFORMATION **RESOURCE CARD** **53**

SURVEY

ANALYZE THE RESULTS OF THE STUDY

STEPS:

1. Look back at the questions asked at the beginning of the survey and write these on paper.

2. Tally (count the answers) the information from the questionnaire in several ways in order to answer all the questions.

3. Write an answer for each of the questions.

4. Think about other questions that may have come to mind that you wonder about and might like to answer at another time.

Example of a survey on the next card...

© Johnsen and Johnson, 1986

LESSON 21: COLLECT INFORMATION: NOTE TAKING

Concepts: 1. Note taking
                 2. Main idea
                 3. Outline

Objective: Students will record important information from a source in one form of note taking.

Materials: 1. Newspapers or magazine articles
                 2. Resource Cards 56, 57, 58, 59, 60
                 3. Teacher's Guide, Lessons 17 and 22
                 4. Chalkboard and/or overhead

Evaluation: Given resources, are the.students able to record important information in one form of note taking?

Note to Teacher:

The students will need to have the skills of outlining (see **Lesson 22, Teacher's Guide**) and /or classifying (see **Lesson 17, Teacher's Guide**) before they are ready to take notes. Be sure to preassess these areas.

Procedure:

1. Explain the purpose of taking notes on material read or heard: it is a method of recording important information you have collected from books, magazine, films, interviews or any other source (see **Resource Card 56**).

2. Pass out note cards, resources to be used for taking notes, and pencils.

3. List on the chalkboard or overhead, "*Before* Note Taking." Write these steps (see **Resource Card 57**).

   • Have materials ready.

   • Scan the materials. Decide how you want to take notes.

   • Write on your paper or note card the title, author, publisher, city of publication, date and page numbers.

3. Show the students one of the resources that you have. Show them where to find the information to include on the notecard. Prepare a note card on the overhead or chalkboard. Have the students tell you whether or not you have included all of the information.

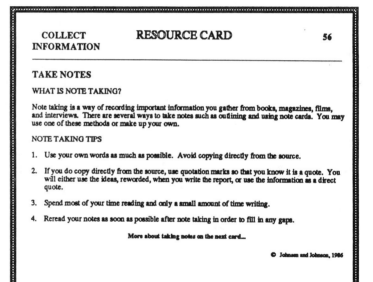

COLLECT INFORMATION   **RESOURCE CARD**   56

TAKE NOTES

WHAT IS NOTE TAKING?

Note taking is a way of recording important information you gather from books, magazines, films, and interviews. There are several ways to take notes such as outlining and using note cards. You may use one of these methods or make up your own.

NOTE TAKING TIPS

1. Use your own words as much as possible. Avoid copying directly from the source.

2. If you do copy directly from the source, use quotation marks so that you know it is a quote. You will either use the ideas, reworded, when you write the report, or use the information as a direct quote.

3. Spend most of your time reading and only a small amount of time writing.

4. Reread your notes as soon as possible after note taking in order to fill in any gaps.

More about taking notes on the next card...

© Johnson and Johnson, 1986

Procedure:

4. Now have the students prepare one of their note cards using the information in their resource. As each is finished, have several read what they have written at the top of their note cards. Continue in this fashion until all of the students appear to understand how to prepare a note card.

5. List on the chalkboard or overhead "*During* note taking." Write these steps (see **Resource Card 57**):

   • Write down headings, main ideas and supporting details.

   • Use abbreviations.

   • Put "?'s" when you don't understand something or need more information.

   • Use symbols to emphasize important information.

   • Cross out; don't waste time erasing.

   • Find important information by looking for signal words.

6. Now write these note taking tips on the chalkboard/overhead or have a copy for each student. Discuss each one.

   • Use your own words as much as possible. Avoid copying directly from a source.

   • If you copy directly from a source, use quotation marks so that you will know it is a quote.

   • When you use the information in your report, use the ideas, but write them in your own words. If you use the information as a direct quote, make sure that you credit the author (*i.e.,* write the author's name beside the quote).

   • Most of your time will be spent reading and a small amount of time will be spent writing.

COLLECT INFORMATION   **RESOURCE CARD**   57

TAKE NOTES

HOW DO I TAKE NOTES?

1. Before note taking

   • Have materials ready--paper or note cards and pencil.
   • Look over the material you will be studying and decide how you want to take notes--outlining, note cards or your own method.
   • Always list the source on your paper or note card--title of source, author, publisher, city of publication, date.

2. During note taking

   • Use headings or main topics.
   • Use abbreviations.
   • Put "?s" when you don't understand something or need more information.
   • Use symbols to emphasize important information, such as underline, circles or check marks.
   • This is a rough draft, so don't waste time erasing. Cross out.
   • Look for signal words for clues about important information (see back of this card).

Example is on the back...

© Johnson and Johnson, 1986

57b

TAKE NOTES

EXAMPLES OF SIGNAL WORDS:

Support Signals		Conclusion Signals
for example	another	therefore
for instance	also	finally
first, second, third	furthermore	in conclusion
similarly	likewise	as a result
most important	in addition	in summary
a major development	equally important	from this we see
again, next, then	whereas	hence
furthermore	consequently	thus

More about taking notes on the next card...

© Johnson and Johnson, 1986

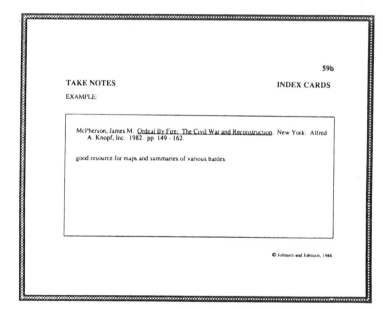

COLLECT
INFORMATION **RESOURCE CARD** 59

TAKE NOTES INDEX CARD

HOW DO I USE AN INDEX CARD?

STEPS:

1. Write the study question at the top of each index card.

2. Select a book, chapter or film from which to take notes.

3. List the following information on the index card:

    *   title of book, chapter, film (or source)
    *   author
    *   publisher (city: name of publishing company)
    *   copyright date
    *   page numbers where information was found

4. Write any information on the card that pertains to the study question or note a particular aspect of the book. You may find many pieces of interesting information, but list only the information that helps to answer the study question.

Example is on the back...

© Johnsen and Johnson, 1986

59b

TAKE NOTES INDEX CARDS

EXAMPLE:

McPherson, James M. Ordeal By Fire: The Civil War and Reconstruction. New York: Alfred A. Knopf, Inc. 1982. pp. 149 - 162.

good resource for maps and summaries of various battles

© Johnsen and Johnson, 1986

COLLECT
INFORMATION **RESOURCE CARD** 60

TAKE NOTES OUTLINE

HOW DO I OUTLINE?

STEPS:

1. Select a book, chapter, film or your notes to outline.

2. Determine the main ideas. They will be written beside the Roman numerals.

3. List the first main idea beside *I*.

4. List supporting ideas under *I* beside *A.*, *B.*, *C.* and so on. Always indent the letters.

5. Continue this procedure for *II* with the second main idea.

6. Use words and phrases, not sentences.

7. If you will be researching other sources, you may leave space to fill in later.

Example is on the back...

© Johnsen and Johnson, 1986

Procedure:

7. Have one of the students read a paragraph aloud from one of your resources as you take notes on the overhead or chalkboard . (Use the index card format first.) Be sure to include all of the steps listed. At the end of your note taking, have the students tell you what steps you used in taking notes.

8. Now have one of the students read another paragraph aloud from one of your resources. Again, take notes on the overhead or chalkboard. (Use the outline card format.) Again, be sure to include all of the steps listed. At the end of your note taking, have the students tell you what steps you used in taking notes.

9. Point out the two different formats for taking notes: index card (see **Resource Card 59**) and outlining (see **Resource Card 60**).

10. Tell them that they may use either format.

11. Now have one of the students read another paragraph aloud from one of your resources. This time, when you are taking notes on the overhead or chalkboard, do not include all of the steps listed. At the end of your note taking, have the students tell what steps you used and which ones you did not use.

12. If the students appear to understand how to take notes, divide them into groups of two and have one in each pair read aloud from one of their resources while the other takes notes; then reverse. If not, continue modeling the note taking procedure with those that need more assistance.

13. While the students are taking notes. Walk around the room and assist those who may be having difficulty.

Procedure:

14. When the students are finished, talk about what they did, using each step:

    • What were some of your main headings? supporting ideas?

    • What abbreviations did you use?

    • What questions did you have?

    • What symbols did you use in emphasizing important information?

    • Did you cross out information?

    • What signal words did you find in your resource?

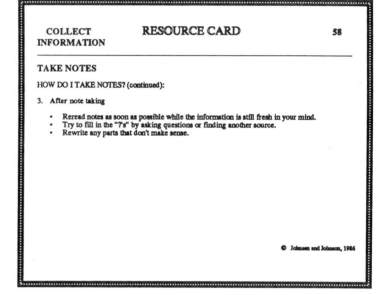

15. Discuss the areas in which they encountered difficulty and have other students provide suggestions.

16. Discuss what students should do *after* taking notes (see **Resource Card 58**).

    • Reread notes as soon as possible while the information is still fresh in your mind. Make sure that you understand what your notes say.

    • Try to answer the "?'s" by going to another source.

    • Rewrite the parts in your notes that don't make sense.

17. **ASSIGNMENT**: Have the students take notes from resources they are using.

LESSON 22:   COLLECT INFORMATION: NOTE TAKING--OUTLINING

Concepts: 1. Outline
2. Main idea
3. Subtopic
4. Details

Objective: Students will place information from resources in outline form using main ideas, subtopics and details.

Materials: 1. Newspapers, magazine articles, or books
2. Resource Card 60
3. OH Transparencies 3, 4, and 5
4. Chalkboard and overhead

Evaluation: Given resources, are the students able to place information in outline form using main ideas, subtopics and details?

Note to Teacher:

The students should be able to identify main ideas and classify before outlining.

Procedure:

1. Explain the purpose of an outline: an outline helps you place ideas and thoughts into an organized format. Outlines may contain titles, main ideas, subtopics and details. Subtopics support the main ideas while details support the subtopics.

2. Put **OH Trasparency 3** on the overhead. Show them this example. Point out the title (*i.e.*, "Yachts"), the main ideas (*i.e,* "History," "Current yachts," "Races"), the subtopics (*i.e.*, "Early commercial uses," "Early Sporting Uses," *etc.*) and the details (*i.e.*, "Revenue marine," "Privateers," "Slavery," *etc.*).

3. Show them another outline (see **Resource Card 60**). Again point out the title, the main ideas and the subtopics.

OH3
YACHTS

I. History

   A. Early commercial uses

      1. Revenue marine
      2. Privateers
      3. Slavery

   B. Early sporting uses

      1. World's Fair of 1851
      2. New York Yacht Club

II. Current yachts

   A. Daysailers

      1. Characteristics
      2. Use

   B. Offshore ocean racers

      1. Characteristics
      2. Use

III. Races

   A. "One-design" race

      1. Boat specifications
      2. Location

   B. "Handicap" race

      1. Handicap specifications
      2. Location

106   © Johnson and Johnson, 1986

Procedure:

4. Show them other outlines from books and resources that you might have. Ask the students how all of the outlines are alike. List these likenesses on the chalkboard. Some of the likenesses might be:

   - Have a title
   - Have Roman numerals, capital letters, small letters, arabic numerals, arabic numerals in parentheses
   - Same sort of numeral, letter, *etc.* lined up under one another
   - First letters capitalized
   - Have similar form beside letters and numerals
   - Subtopics support main ideas; details support subtopics

5. Now ask the students how the outlines are different. List these differences on the chalkboard. Some of the differences might be:

   - Number of Roman numerals, arabic numerals, letters, parenthesis
   - The format of what is written beside each letter and/or numeral (*i.e.*, some may be in sentence form, some in phrases, some in questions, *etc.*).
   - The content or subject matter

6. Put **OH Transparency 4** on the overhead. Put the following *titles* (**or ones that the students may be interested in**) on the Title Lines: *Space, Machines*. Now put these *words* (**or ones that are related to the topic of interest**) in the blank spaces at the side of **OH Transparency 4** under *words*: *Inclined plane, Planets, Lever, Pulley, Stars, Wheel and axel*. Ask the students which of the main ideas would go under which titles. Place the different names under the correct title lines (Answers: Machines--Inclined plane, Lever, Pulley, Wheel and axel; Space--Planets, Stars).

7. Tell them that if the main idea is correct it can be used with the title to make a sentence. Say, "A lever is a machine; a pulley is a machine." Prove each outline in the same way.

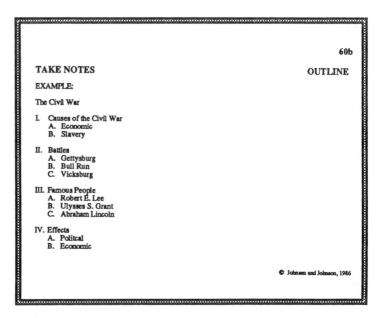

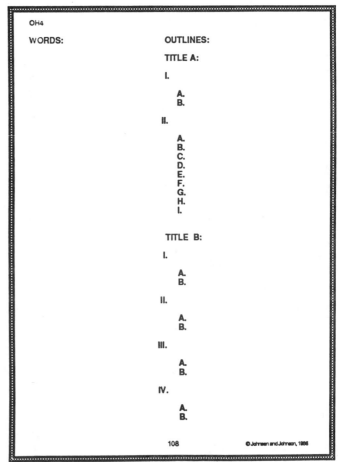

```
OH4--OUTLINING

WORDS:                          OUTLINES:

                                TITLE A:  Space

                                  I.  Stars

                                        A. Sun
                                        B. Constellations

                                  II. Planets

                                        A. Mercury
                                        B. Venus
                                        C. Mars
                                        D. Earth
                                        E. Saturn
                                        F. Uranus
                                        G. Pluto
                                        H. Neptune
                                        I. Jupiter


                                TITLE B:  Machines

                                  I.  Inclined Plane

                                        A. Parts
                                        B. Uses

                                  II. Lever

                                        A. Parts
                                        B. Uses

                                  III. Pulley

                                        A. Parts
                                        B. Uses

                                  IV. Wheel and axel

                                        A. Parts
                                        B. Uses
```

Procedure:

8. Now divide the students into groups. Have them read the same selection (or read a selection to the entire class). Have each group write down the main ideas of the selection. Then have each group share the main ideas that they wrote down. Assist the groups in writing the main ideas in the same form (*i.e.*, questions, phrases, sentences) and in placing them beside the Roman numerals in a column fashion. Have the groups leave room under each one for subtopics and details.

9. Now erase the words at the side of **OH Transparency 4** Place these subtopics in the empty space: *Earth, Mercury, What are its parts?, Mars, Jupiter, Constellations, Pluto, Uranus, How is it used?, Venus, Neptune, Saturn, Sun.* Ask the students which subtopics would go under which main ideas (**Answers: see example**). (They will discover that they can use a subtopic under more than one main idea.)

10. Tell them that if the subtopic is correct, it can be used with the main idea to make a sentence. For example, say, "What are the parts of an inclined plane?; What are the uses of an inclined plane?"

11. Now reread the selection from Step #8. This time have the groups write down the subtopics under each of their main ideas. Have them check their subtopics by making sentences with their subtopics and main ideas. Have each group share the subtopics they wrote. Again assist the groups in writing the subtopics in the same form and in placing the subtopics beside the correct capital letters.

Procedure:

12. Now place these details on the chalkboard: *Size, Automobile, Distance from the Sun, Moving companies, Wheels, Topography, Sattelites, Orion, Composition, Leo, Elevators, Scorpio, Grooved wheel, Ursa Minor, Plane, Support (bricks), Cable railway, Axis, Bar, Changing tires, Making see-saws, Ski Lift, Steering wheels, Line, Bar.* Put **OH Transparency 5** on the overhead. Ask the students which details would go under which subtopics (**Possible answers: see example**). Place these details beside each numeral. (They may discover that they may use a detail under more than one subtopic.)

13. Tell them that if the detail is correct, it can be used with the subtopic to make a sentence. For example, say, "An inclined plane is used in cable railways and in moving furniture; Pluto may be described by its size, distance from the sun and topography."

14. Now reread the selection from Step #8. This time have the groups write down the details under each of their subtopics. Have each group check their details by making sentences with their subtopics and main ideas. Have each group share the details they wrote. Again assist each group in writing the details in the same form and in placing the details beside the correct number.

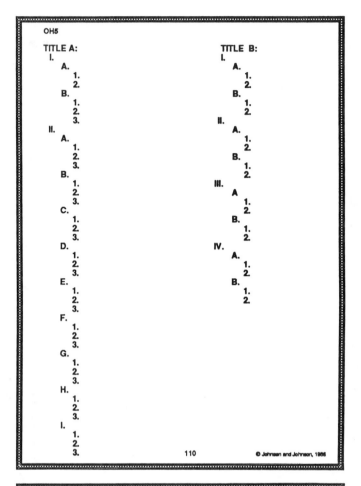

TITLE A: Space

I. Stars
  A. Sun
    1. Composition
    2. Size
  B. Constellations
    1. Orion
    2. Leo
    3. Scorpio
II. Planets
  A. Mercury
    1. Size
    2. Distance from the Sun
    3. Topography
  B. Venus
    1. Size
    2. Distance from the Sun
    3. Topography
  C. Mars
    1. Size
    2. Distance from the Sun
    3. Topography
  D. Earth
    1. Size
    2. Distance from the Sun
    3. Topography
  E. Saturn
    1. Size
    2. Distance from the Sun
    3. Topography
  F. Uranus
    1. Size
    2. Distance from the Sun
    3. Topography
  G. Pluto
    1. Size
    2. Distance from the Sun
    3. Topography
  H. Neptune
    1. Size
    2. Distance from the Sun
    3. Topography
  I. Jupiter
    1. Size
    2. Distance from the Sun
    3. Topography

TITLE B: Machines

I. Lever
  A. What are its parts?
    1. Axis
    2. Bar
  B. How is it used?
    1. Changing tires
    2. Making see-saws
II. Inclined plane
  A. What are its parts?
    1. Plane
    2. Support
  B. How is it used?
    1. Cable railway
    2. Moving furniture
III. Pulley
  A. What are its parts?
    1. Grooved wheel
    2. Line
  B. How is it used?
    1. Elevators
    2. Ski lift
IV. Wheel and axel
  A. What are its parts?
    1. Wheels
    2. Bar
  B. How is it used?
    1. Automobiles
    2. Steering wheels

OH5

```
┌─────────────────────────────────────────────────────┐
│                                                       │
│   COLLECT            RESOURCE CARD              60     │
│   INFORMATION                                         │
│  ─────────────────────────────────────────────────   │
│   TAKE NOTES                              OUTLINE     │
│   HOW DO I OUTLINE?                                   │
│   STEPS:                                              │
│   1. Select a book, chapter, film or your notes to outline. │
│   2. Determine the main ideas. They will be written beside the Roman numerals. │
│   3. List the first main idea beside I.               │
│   4. List supporting ideas under I beside A., B., C. and so on. Always indent the letters. │
│   5. Continue this procedure for II with the second main idea. │
│   6. Use words and phrases, not sentences.            │
│   7. If you will be researching other sources, you may leave space to fill in later. │
│                                                       │
│                   Example is on the back...           │
│                                      © Johnson and Johnson, 1986 │
│                                                       │
└─────────────────────────────────────────────────────┘
```

Procedure:

15. Put **Resource Card 60** on the overhead to review the steps in outlining. Have the students share what they have learned about outlining.

16. Summarize with the following points:

    - An outline divides a subject into its **major** parts.

    - These parts are organized into a sequence.

    - The grammatic form of the outline may be in topics, phrases or sentences although the form should be consistent within each division.

    - Subdivisions should have at least two sections (*i.e.*, "A" should have "B," "1" should have "2," *etc.*).

    - In checking the form of your outline, you should be able to make sentences with the topics, subtopics and details.

17. **ASSIGNMENT**. Have the students take notes in outline form from one of their resources. You might want to have them only outline main ideas first; check these. Then have them outline the subtopics under these main ideas; check these. Finally, have them fill in the details as needed.

LESSON 23:   COLLECT INFORMATION: WRITE LETTERS

Concepts: 1. Letter
                   2. Address
                   3. Salutation
                   4. Complementary close

Objective: Students will be able to write business letters requesting information, an interview and/or permission to make a visit.

Materials: 1. Example letters and envelopes
                   2. Resource Cards 61, 62
                   3. OH Transparency 6
                   4. Stationery and envelopes
                   5. Chalkboard and overhead

Evaluation: Given a person or company to write, are the students able to write business letters requesting information, an interview and/or permission to make a visit?

Procedure:

1. Explain the purpose of writing a business letter: letters are used to request an interview, information or permission to make a visit (see **Resource Card 61**).

2. Show examples of letters (see **Resource Card 62 and OH Transparency 6**). If students brought letters, have them show their examples. Point out the differences between a business letter and a personal letter.

3. Ask the students how all of the letters are alike.   List these likenesses on the chalkboard or overhead:

   • Have return address
   • Have a date
   • Have business' address
   • Have greeting or salutation
   • Have a text
   • Have a complementary close
   • Have a signature
   • Sequence of items
   • Have a colon after the greeting
   • Have a comma after the complementary close
   • Have a typed name under the signature

COLLECT INFORMATION	RESOURCE CARD	61

WRITE LETTERS

WHY SHOULD I WRITE LETTERS?

Letters are used to request information, an interview or permission to make a visit.
Letter writers should be familiar with the proper form in order to create a good impression.

STEPS:

1. Write your address.
2. Write the date.
3. Write the name and address of the person or company from which you wish to get information.
4. Begin the letter with a greeting.
5. Tell the person who you are and why you are writing.
6. Request the information needed.
7. Thank the person for the help.
8. End the letter with a closing.
9. Sign the letter.
10. Have the teacher proofread the letter and rewrite the letter as needed.

Example form is on the back...

© Johnsen and Johnson, 1986

61b

WRITE LETTERS

EXAMPLE FORM:

(Your Address)
(Date)

(Inside Address)

(Salutation)

(Text of Letter)

(Complementary Close)
(Your Signature)

Example of letter is on the next card...
© Johnsen and Johnson, 1986

OH6

James DeMesquita
Glendale Elementary
24 Congress Avenue
Glendale, OH 45246

October 31, 1986

Ms. Molly Lee
Green Thumb Nursery
15 Maple Circle
Cincinnati, OH 45246

Dear Ms. Lee:

I am working on an Independent study project about plants in my fourth grade class. I would like to visit your nursery and learn about the plants that are natural to Ohio. Please let me know if there might be a time that would be convenient to come visit.

I look forward to hearing from you.

Sincerely,

James DeMesquita

P.S. I am particularly interested in wildflowers.

cc. Mr. Masters, Teacher
     Mrs. Sussman, Principal

112   © Johnson and Johnson, 1986

COLLECT INFORMATION	RESOURCE CARD	62

WRITE LETTERS   EXAMPLE

7 Jefferson Avenue
Austin, Texas 78703
February 2, 1986

Artificial Intelligence Laboratory
45 West Street
New York, New York 10013

Dear Sir or Madam:

I am working on a special project in my seventh grade science class on the topic of robotics. I understand that your laboratory is doing research on robotics and I would like to have any information you have on this subject. I would appreciate your sending me materials and information that would assist me in the study of robotics.

Thank you for any help that you can give me.

Sincerely,

Example of an envelope form is on the back...

© Johnson and Johnson, 1986

Procedure:

4. Ask the students how the letters are different:

    - Return address in the letterhead
    - Name of person or company not known
    - Courtesy title (*i.e.*, Mr., Mrs., Ms., Dr., Professor)
    - Paragraphs in block format or indented
    - Number of paragraphs
    - Title under the name at the complementary close
    - Enclosures
    - Carbon copies (*i.e.*, cc:)
    - P.S.
    - Initials of author and typist (SJ:dy)

NOTE: You may wish to model only the type of letter that the students will be writing (*i.e.*, requesting information, an interview, or a visit).

5. Now model a letter for requesting information. Write the letter on the overhead or chalkboard. You may wish to use one of the student's requests for topic information in your example (see **Resource Card 62** for an example).

6. Now model a letter requesting an interview. Again, write the letter on the overhead or chalkboard. You may wish to use one of the student's requests for an interview in your example. Your text might be similar to **Resource Card 62**, changing sentences two and three in the first paragraph and the final sentence: "I have heard that you have much expertise in the area of robotics, and I would like to request an interview. Please let me know if there might be a time that would be convenient for you. I look forward to any help that you may be able to give me."

Procedure:

7. Now model a letter requesting a visit. Again, write the letter on the overhead or chalkboard. You may wish to use one of the student's requests for an interview in your example. Your text might be similar to **Resource Card 62,** changing sentences two and three in the first paragraph and the final sentence: "I would like to visit your laboratory to gain more information. Please let me know if there might be a time that would be convenient for this visit. I look forward to any help that you may be able to give me."

8. Break the students into groups as needed: those who will be writing letters for information; those who will be writing letters for visits; those who will be writing letters for interviews.

9. Have the students write their letters. Stress that these letters will be their rough drafts. Assist each group as needed.

10. Have the groups share their letters.

11. Now show the group examples of envelopes (see the back of **Resource Card 62**). Ask the students how these envelopes are similar:

    • Sender's address in the upper left hand corner
    • The name and address of the company in the center of the envelope
    • The stamp in the upper right hand corner
    • The name, address, and city in a block format

12. Ask the students how these envelopes are different:

    • Letterhead used
    • Name of person in company known
    • Additions to envelope made (*i.e*, attention, confidential, *etc.*)

13. Have the students write a draft of the envelopes they will use for their letters.

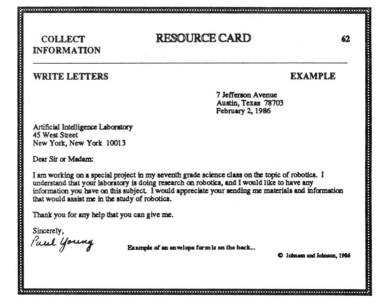

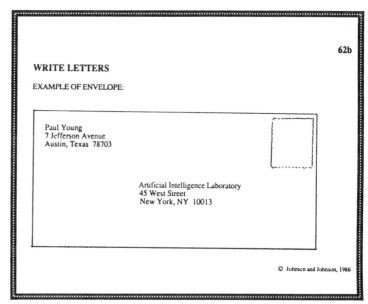

Procedure:

14. After you have checked both letter and envelope drafts, have the students transfer the information over to stationery and envelopes that they will be sending.

15. Review the steps for writing a letter (see **Resource Card 61**).

    - Write your address.
    - Write the date.
    - Write the name and address of the person or company from which you wish to get information.
    - Begin the letter with a greeting.
    - Tell the person who you are and why you are writing.
    - Request the information needed.
    - Thank the person for the help.
    - End the letter with a closing.
    - Sign the letter.
    - Have the teacher proofread the letter and rewrite the letter as needed.

    Emphasize that letters should be neat and in proper form to create a good impression.

16. **ASSIGNMENT:** Send the letters to the persons and/or businesses.

Whatever you vividly imagine, ardently desire, sincerely believe, and enthusiastically act upon must inevitably come to pass.

P. J. Meyer

LESSON 24.   OVERVIEW

Concepts: 1. Product
                     2. Product plan

Objective: Students will select and develop a product which answers the questions about the
                     topic studied.

Materials: 1. Resource Cards 63-92
                     2. Student Booklet, pages 3, 16, 17, 18, 19, 20
                     3. Teacher Guide, Lesson 2
                     4. Chalkboard and/or overhead

Evaluation: Did the students select and develop a product that answered the questions about their topics?

(**Note for Group Independent Study**: If you would like all of the students to develop the same type of product,
follow the procedure listed in Step 4.)

Procedure:

1.   Explain to the students that the main
     purpose of developing a product is to share
     information they have learned in the best
     possible way. The product should answer
     the study questions (see **Resource Card
     64**).

2.   Have the students look in the **Student
     Booklets, page 16**. Read the definition
     of a product. Name several examples of
     products (*e.g.*, a book, a filmstrip, *etc.*).
     Now have the students brainstorm possible
     products. Have them list these at the
     bottom of page 16. (You may want to use
     those that are listed on **Resource Card
     65**.)

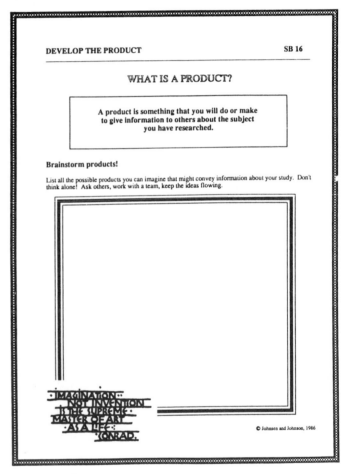

DEVELOP THE PRODUCT   SB 16

WHAT IS A PRODUCT?

A product is something that you will do or make
to give information to others about the subject
you have researched.

Brainstorm products!

List all the possible products you can imagine that might convey information about your study. Don't
think alone! Ask others, work with a team, keep the ideas flowing.

IMAGINATION
NOT INVENTION
IS THE SUPREME
MASTER OF ART
AS A LIFE.
CONRAD.

© Johnsen and Johnson, 1986

DEVELOP THE   RESOURCE CARD   63
PRODUCT

PRODUCT INDEX

PRODUCT	CARDS
Book	66 - 69
Diagram	70 - 73
Diorama	74
Filmstrip	75
Game	76 - 77
Graph	78 - 83
Poster	84
Puppet Show	85 - 86
Report	87 - 88
Tape Recording	89
T. V. Show	90
Timeline	91 - 92

© Johnsen and Johnson, 1986

DEVELOP THE PRODUCT   RESOURCE CARD   64

INTRODUCTION

WHAT IS A PRODUCT?

A product is something that you do or make to give information to others about the subject you have researched.

HOW DO I DEVELOP A PRODUCT?

1. Look at the Product Sampler on the next card or the Index on the previous card to decide which of the products would best allow you to present your information to others.

2. Select the best product and use the Resource Cards to help you develop the product.

© Johnson and Johnson, 1986

DEVELOP THE PRODUCT   RESOURCE CARD   65

PRODUCT SAMPLER

A   advertisement, advice column, album, allegory, analogy, anecdote, animation, annotated bibliography, artifact, audio tape, audition, autobiography
B   ballet, banner, batik, bibliography, billboard, biography, book, book binding technique, building, bulletin board, button
C   cartoon, calendar, calligraphy, campaign, case study, catalog, chart, code, collage, collection, comedy act, community service, composition, computer program, conference, costume, crossword puzzle, cook book
D   dance, debate, demonstration, design, diagram, diorama, discovery, display, drama, drawing
E   editorial, energy saver, equipment, etching, experiment, explanation
F   fashion, feature story, festival, film, filmstrip, fiction, flag, flannel board, food,
G   gadget, gallery, game, gift, graph, graphic design, greeting card, garden
H   handbook, help service, hieroglyphic, historical report, hologram, holograph, "hot line" service
I   icon, index, inscription, instrument, interview, invention
J   jamboree, jewelry design, jazz composition, jigsaw puzzle, joke, jokebook, journal
K   kaleidescope, kit, knitting pattern, kite

More products are on the back...

© Johnson and Johnson, 1986

PRODUCT SAMPLER (continued)   65b

L   label, laboratory, ladder tournament, language (new), layout design, learning center, ledger, letter to editor, library, life list (birdwatchers), lithograph, log, lyrics
M   magazine, magic trick, map, marquee, mask, menu, mobile, model, mnemonic device, movie, mural, museum display, musical instrument, musical production, mime
N   newsletter, newspaper, news story, notice, novel, number system
O   oath, observation record, oil color, opera, orchestra arrangement, origami, outline
P   painting, pamphlet, paper marbling, papier maché, parody, pattern, pennant, petition, photograph, play, poem, poster, press conference, puppet show, puzzle
Q   query, question, questionnaire, quilling, quilt, quiz
R   radio program, recipe, report, review, robot, role play, round robin tournament
S   satire, scrapbook, screenplay, script, sculpture, shadow box, short story, silk screen, simulation, skit, slide show, song, speech, survey, stage set
T   tape recording, technique, tee shirt design, television show, tepee, term paper, test, theme, theory, time line, tool, tour guide, tournament, transparency, travelogue
U   uncial script, uniform, unit of study, update, urn, utility
V   verse, video tape, vignette, visual aid, visual casette recording, volunteer program
W   walking tour, wall hanging, water color, weather map, weaving, whittling, wire sculpture, woodcarving, woodwork, word game
X   xerographic print, x-ray, xylograph
Y   yarn (story), yearbook, yodel, yurt
Z   zodiac, zoographic study, zoological project

© Johnson and Johnson, 1986

Procedure:

3. If you have products that other students have developed, you might share these with the students.

4. If you want the students to develop a similar type of product, follow these steps:

A. Show products from the **Resource Cards 66-92** with the students (see the pages following this lesson for product examples).

B. Talk about the questions that the group or individual students asked in their studies. Decide which products would best answer these questions. Write these on the chalkboard.

C. Talk about the audience that will be viewing or hearing about the product. Decide which products would be best for this audience. Write these on the chalkboard.

That's what education means, to be able to do what you've never done before

A.F. Palmer

Procedure:

D. Have the students look in the **Student Booklets, page 17.** Review the steps of evaluation (see **Teacher Guide, Lesson 2, page 5**).

E. From the list on the chalkboard, select five products to evaluate. Have the students list these in the **Student Booklets, page 18.** Now have the students evaluate the products.

F. Have them check the product they have selected on their product plans in their **student booklets, page 3.** Next to the "final product" write the due date.

DEVELOP THE PRODUCT   **SB 17**

HOW DO I SELECT THE BEST PRODUCT?

1. On the lines beside "A," "B," and "C", list some possible products you are considering (see example).

2. By the numbers, list some reasons why you might develop a product.

3. Look at the first reason and put a "3" in the box next to the product that best fits the reason. Put a "2" for the product that fits next best, and "1" for the product that fits least best.

4. Add the digits in each product column and enter the sum in the "Total" column. The product with the *largest* number should be the first choice, or the best product for the project.

EXAMPLE:

PRODUCT EVALUATION CHART

C. Which will give the audience the most information?

QUESTIONS   B. Which will be the most interesting for me?

A. Which will be the most unusual?

T O T A L

PRODUCTS	A	B	C	
1. book (illustrated)				
2. written report with graph				
3. oral report with display				
4. board game				
5. chart of survey results				

adapted from *Texas Future Problem Solving*

© Johnsen & Johnson, 1986

DEVELOP THE PRODUCT   **SB 18**

PRODUCT EVALUATION CHART

Complete the following chart to help you select the best product. List three evaluation questions beside A, B, C, and products you are evaluating beside the numbers. Rank order the best product for each reason, with "1" as the highest score. Remember, the *highest* score should be the best product for you to develop. Follow example on SB17.

C. _____

QUESTIONS   B. _____

A. _____

T O T A L

PRODUCTS	A	B	C	
1.				
2.				
3.				
4.				
5.				

adapted from *Texas Future Problem Solving*

© Johnsen & Johnson, 1986

DEVELOP A PRODUCT

DEVELOP THE PRODUCT   SB 19

WHAT IS A PRODUCT PLAN?

A product plan is a system used in
planning and developing the product.

The plan should include:

1. a list of steps to follow to complete the product
2. all materials needed to develop the product
3. an approximate amount of time needed for each step.

In the space below, draw a sketch of how you want your final product to look.

© Johnsen & Johnson, 1986

DEVELOP THE PRODUCT   SB 20

PRODUCT PLAN

Complete the chart below, filling in steps you need to follow in order to develop the product.

STEPS   TIME NEEDED

MATERIALS NEEDED

PLEASE..
DON'T SUPPLY
ANY MORE
INFORMATION.

I'M ALREADY
TOO WELL
INFORMED :

© Johnsen and Johnson, 1986

Procedure:

G. Have the students turn to **page 19** in the **Student Booklets**. Discuss the product plan and the steps that should be included.

H. Show them an example of the product that they have selected from the Resource Cards or ones that other students have done.

I. At the bottom of **page 19** in the **Student Booklets,** have the students draw sketches of how they want their final products to look. You might want to draw this sketch together, using the chalkboard.

J. When they are finished with their sketches, have them look in the **Student Booklets, page 20.**

K. Have them "think through" the steps needed for their products and/or use the ones from the **Resource Cards.**

L. Have the students write these steps in the **Student Booklets, page 20.**

M. Help the students estimate the time for each step. Write this time next to each step on **page 20.** See if the total time needed will be sufficient in completing the product by the due date. If not, the product may need to be modified or changed. (You might want them to write down the "real" amount of time that it takes them to complete that step as they work on their products and compare the estimate with this time.)

N. Examine each step with the students and write down the materials needed on **page 20.**

O. Have the students bring these materials from home or help them locate these materials from school and/or local businesses.

Procedure:

4. If you want the students to develop different products, follow these steps:

A. Show products from the **Resource Cards 66-92** with the students (see the pages following this lesson for product examples).

B. Talk about the questions that the group or individual students asked in their studies. Decide which products would best answer these questions. Write these on the chalkboard.

C. Talk about the audience that will be viewing or hearing about the product. Decide which products would be best for this audience. Write these on the chalkboard.

D. Have the students look in the **Student Booklets, page 17**. Review the steps of evaluation (see **Teacher Guide, Lesson 2, page 5**).

E. From the list on the chalkboard, have each student select five products to evaluate. Have each student list these in the **Student Booklet, page 18**. Now have each student evaluate the products as an assignment.

F. Set aside a block of time to meet with each student for five minutes. During this time, discuss the product chosen and make sure that the product answers the questions and is appropriate for the audience. Have them check the selected product on their product plans in the **Student Booklet, page 3**. Next to the "final product" write the due date.

G. Group students according to their products. Have each group turn to **page 19 in the Student Booklets**. Discuss the product plan and the steps that should be included.

H. Show each group an example of the product that they have selected from the Resource Cards or ones that other students have done.

I. Have each group draw sketches of how they want their final products to look at the bottom of **page 19** in the Student Booklets.

J. When they are finished with their sketches, have each group look at page 20 in the Student Booklets.

K. Have each group "think through" the steps needed for their products and/or use the ones from the **Resource Cards**.

L. Have each group write these steps on **page 20** in the **Student Booklets**.

M. Help each group estimate the time for each step. Write this time next to each step on **page 20**. See if the total time needed will be sufficient in completing the product by the due date. If not, the product may need to be modified or changed. (You might want them to write down the "real" amount of time that it takes them to complete that step as they work on their products and compare the estimate with this time.)

N. Examine each step with each group and write down the materials needed on **page 20**.

O. Have each group bring these materials from home or help them locate these materials from school and/or local businesses.

6. **ASSIGNMENT:** Have the students work on their products. You will need to monitor this phase carefully and/or set up "peer helpers" who have special skills in product development.

NOTE: Examples from Resource Cards for different products may be found on these Teacher Guide (TG) pages:

Book, TG 82-83; *Diagram*, TG 83-84; *Diorama*, TG 84; *Flmstrip*, TG 84; *Game*, TG 85; *Graph*, TG 85-87; *Poster*, TG 87; *Puppet Show*, TG 88; *Report*, TG 88; *Tape Recording*, TG 89; *Television Show*, TG 89; *Time Line*, TG 90

HOW TO DEVELOP A BOOK

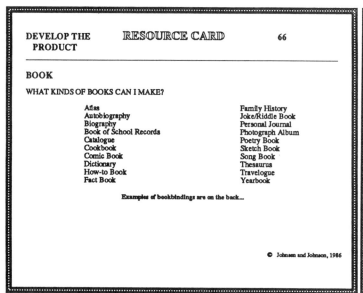

DEVELOP THE PRODUCT — RESOURCE CARD — 66

BOOK

WHAT KINDS OF BOOKS CAN I MAKE?

Atlas	Family History
Autobiography	Joke/Riddle Book
Biography	Personal Journal
Book of School Records	Photograph Album
Catalogue	Poetry Book
Cookbook	Sketch Book
Comic Book	Song Book
Dictionary	Thesaurus
How-to Book	Travelogue
Fact Book	Yearbook

Examples of bookbindings are on the back...

© Johnsen and Johnson, 1986

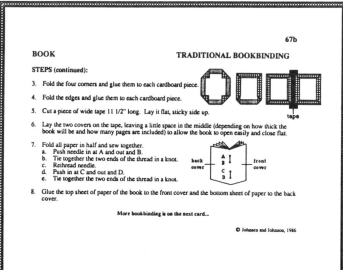

67b

BOOK — **TRADITIONAL BOOKBINDING**

STEPS (continued):

3. Fold the four corners and glue them to each cardboard piece.

4. Fold the edges and glue them to each cardboard piece.

5. Cut a piece of wide tape 11 1/2" long. Lay it flat, sticky side up.

6. Lay the two covers on the tape, leaving a little space in the middle (depending on how thick the book will be and how many pages are included) to allow the book to open easily and close flat.

7. Fold all paper in half and sew together.
   a. Push needle in at A and out and B.
   b. Tie together the two ends of the thread in a knot.
   c. Rethread needle.
   d. Push in at C and out and D.
   e. Tie together the two ends of the thread in a knot.

8. Glue the top sheet of paper of the book to the front cover and the bottom sheet of paper to the back cover.

More bookbinding is on the next card...

© Johnsen and Johnson, 1986

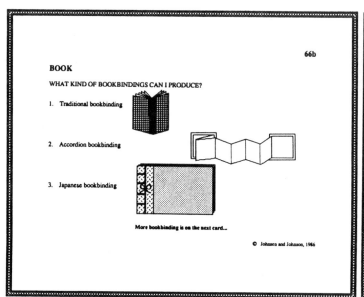

66b

BOOK

WHAT KIND OF BOOKBINDINGS CAN I PRODUCE?

1. Traditional bookbinding

2. Accordion bookbinding

3. Japanese bookbinding

More bookbinding is on the next card...

© Johnsen and Johnson, 1986

DEVELOP THE PRODUCT — RESOURCE CARD — 68

BOOK — **ACCORDION BOOKBINDING**

Materials Needed:
   two pieces of cardboard, each 5 1/2" X 5 1/2"
   Pretty paper or fabric, two pieces each 7" X 7"
   One strip of paper 5" X 30"
   glue or glue stick

STEPS:

1. Center each piece of cardboard on the pretty paper or fabric. (Follow the illustrated example in Steps 2, 3 and 4 of Resource Card 67.)

2. Fold the corners and glue to cardboard.

3. Fold the sides and glue to cardboard.

More steps are on the back...

© Johnsen and Johnson, 1986

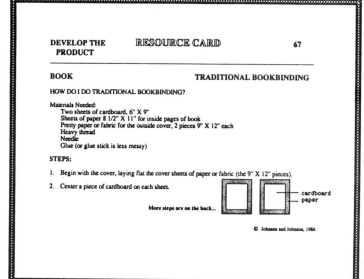

DEVELOP THE PRODUCT — RESOURCE CARD — 67

BOOK — **TRADITIONAL BOOKBINDING**

HOW DO I DO TRADITIONAL BOOKBINDING?

Materials Needed:
   Two sheets of cardboard, 6" X 9"
   Sheets of paper 8 1/2" X 11" for inside pages of book
   Pretty paper or fabric for the outside cover, 2 pieces 9" X 12" each
   Heavy thread
   Needle
   Glue (or glue stick is less messy)

STEPS:

1. Begin with the cover, laying flat the cover sheets of paper or fabric (the 9" X 12" pieces).

2. Center a piece of cardboard on each sheet.

More steps are on the back...

cardboard
paper

© Johnsen and Johnson, 1986

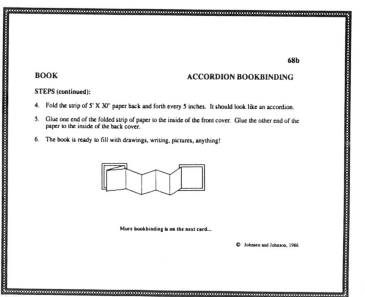

68b

BOOK — **ACCORDION BOOKBINDING**

STEPS (continued):

4. Fold the strip of 5' X 30" paper back and forth every 5 inches. It should look like an accordion.

5. Glue one end of the folded strip of paper to the inside of the front cover. Glue the other end of the paper to the inside of the back cover.

6. The book is ready to fill with drawings, writing, pictures, anything!

More bookbinding is on the next card...

© Johnsen and Johnson, 1986

HOW TO DEVELOP A BOOK AND A DIAGRAM   RESOURCE CARDS 69-72

DEVELOP THE PRODUCT   RESOURCE CARD   **69**

BOOK   **JAPANESE BOOKBINDING**

Materials Needed:
  Two pieces of cardboard, each 5 1/2" X 1 1/2"   Hole punch
  Pretty paper or fabric, two pieces each 7" X 3" for bound spine Glue or glue stick
  Two colored sheets of paper, each 5 1/2" X 8" for outside cover Yarn, 40" long
  Stack of paper for inside of book, as many sheets as desired, 5 1/2" X 8" Embroidery needle

STEPS:

1. Lay 7" X 3" pieces of pretty paper or fabric flat on table, pretty side down. (Follow the illustrated example on Steps 2, 3 and 4 of Resource Card 67.)

2. Center the pieces of cardboard on each sheet of pretty paper.

3. Fold corners and glue to cardboard.

4. Fold sides and glue to cardboard.

5. Measure and mark four even dots down the middle of the covered cardboard.

More steps are on the back...

© Johnson and Johnson, 1986

69b

BOOK   **JAPANESE BOOKBINDING**

STEPS (continued):

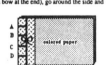

6. Punch holes at each dot.

7. On left side of stack of paper for inside of book, put the top and bottom covered cardboard pieces.

8. Mark the paper where the cover holes are and punch holes in the paper.

9. Thread yard into embroidery needle and sew according to the illustration. Tie a bow on the front when finished.

   Directions for binding:
   Go down at B (keep several inches out in order to tie a bow at the end), go around the side and back down at B.
   Up at A, go around the side and up again at A.
   Go around the top and up again at A.
   Down at B.
   Up at C, go around the side and up again at C.
   Down at D, go around the side and down again at D.
   Go around the bottom and down again at D.
   Up at C. Tie in a Bow.

© Johnson and Johnson, 1986

DEVELOP THE PRODUCT   RESOURCE CARD   **70**

DIAGRAM

WHAT IS A DIAGRAM?

A diagram is a graphic design or drawing that helps to explain something:

  • the parts of an object
  • the steps or stages

© Johnson and Johnson, 1986

DEVELOP THE PRODUCT   RESOURCE CARD   **71**

DIAGRAM

STEPS:

1. Decide what size the drawing should be.

   • Should it be large enought to present in a class presentation?
   • Should it fill a page in a written report?
   • Should it be small enough to insert in the text of a written report?

2. Make a rough sketch of the diagram on a scratch piece of paper.

   • If drawing is difficult for you, trace the picture from a book.
   • If the drawing in the book is too small, use an opaque projector to enlarge it. Ask a teacher for assistance.

3. When you are satisfied with the sketch, draw it again on poster board or good paper.

More steps are on the back...

© Johnson and Johnson, 1986

71b

DIAGRAM

STEPS (continued):

4. Use a ruler and pencil to make lines to the parts of the figure you will explain.

5. Print the words in pencil next to the line.

6. When the diagram is complete, use pens, crayons or felt markers to color it and make it attractive.

© Johnson and Johnson, 1986

DEVELOP THE PRODUCT   RESOURCE CARD   **72**

DIAGRAM   **EXAMPLES**

DIAGRAM OF PARTS

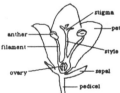

© Johnson and Johnson, 1986

HOW TO DEVELOP A DIAGRAM, A DIORAMA, AND A FILMSTRIP

Card 72b

72b

DIAGRAM　　　　　　　　　　　　　**EXAMPLES**

DIAGRAM OF STAGES

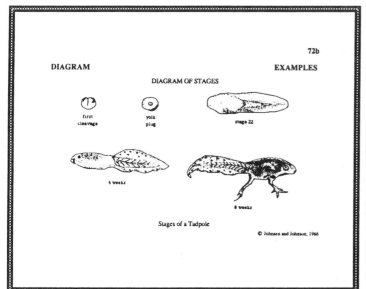

first cleavage　　　yolk plug　　　stage 22

4 weeks

8 weeks

Stages of a Tadpole

© Johnsen and Johnson, 1986

Card 74b

74b

DIORAMA

STEPS:

1. Plan how the diorama will look.
   a. How large is the box? Measure the inside of the box.
   b. What background scene do you want? On scratch paper, make a rough sketch of the background scene to fit the inside of the box.
   c. What objects or models will best depict the scene? Collect or make these.

2. Create the diorama.
   a. Cut paper the same size as the inside of the box.
   b. Draw the background scene from the rough sketch; color or paint it.
   c. When it is dry, glue or tape the scene to the inside of the box.
   d. Arrange the objects or models in the box.

3. Explain what the diorama depicts.
   a. Write a description of the scene to tell others about it.
   b. Label objects or parts, if necessary.

© Johnsen and Johnson, 1986

Card 73

DEVELOP THE PRODUCT　　**RESOURCE CARD**　　**73**

DIAGRAM　　　　　　　　　　　　　**EXAMPLES**

DIAGRAM OF STEPS

born April 7	1975		
		1976	took 1st steps
lived on a farm	1977		
		1978	moved to a new state
brother born	1979		
		1980	started 1st grade
gymnastics team	1981		
		1982	began piano lessons
went to England	1983		
		1984	got a dog

© Johnsen and Johnson, 1986

Card 75

DEVELOP THE PRODUCT　　**RESOURCE CARD**　　**75**

FILMSTRIP

HOW DO I MAKE A FILMSTRIP?

Materials:　　shoe box　　　　permanent felt marker　　　pencil/paper
　　　　　　clear acetate　　　X-acto knife　　　　　　　scotch tape
　　　　　　　　　　　　　　　　　　　　　　　　　　　flashlight

STEPS:

1. Make the box "projector."
   a. Cut out both ends of the shoe box.
   b. With X-acto knife, cut a vertical slit in each side of the box.
   c. Measure the slit.

2. Draw the filmstrip pictures.
   a. Decide what pictures you want to show in the filmstrip and sequence them.
   b. With pencil and paper, draw a rough sketch of each picture side by side, slightly smaller than the size of the slit in the box. Make sure each picture is about as wide as the end of the box.
   c. When you are satisfied with the sketches, draw the pictures on acetate with the felt marker. Either draw or tape pictures side by side so that they will roll through the box projector.

slit

More steps are on the back...

© Johnsen and Johnson, 1986

Card 74

DEVELOP THE PRODUCT　　**RESOURCE CARD**　　**74**

DIORAMA

WHAT IS A DIORAMA?

　　A diorama is a box that contains objects or models that depict a scene.

HOW DO I MAKE A DIORAMA?

Materials Needed:　　cardboard box
　　　　　　　　　paper
　　　　　　　　　paints, crayons, or felt markers
　　　　　　　　　various objects or models

Steps are on the back...

© Johnsen and Johnson, 1986

Card 75b

75b

FILMSTRIP

STEPS (continued):

3. Operate the filmstrip projector.
   a. Slide the acetate filmstrip through both slits in the box.
   b. Point the box projector toward a blank wall.
   c. Place the flashlight behind the picture. The light will project the image onto the wall.
   d. Gently and slowly pull the acetate pictures through the slits. You may want to add music or discuss what the audience is viewing.

© Johnsen and Johnson, 1986

HOW TO DEVELOP A GAME AND A GRAPH   RESOURCE CARDS 76-79

DEVELOP THE PRODUCT   RESOURCE CARD   76

GAME

HOW DO I MAKE A BOARD GAME?

Materials: poster board   box
              pencil and felt markers   dice (optional)
              glue   buttons, paper clips, colored circles
              3" X 5" index cards   various colors of construction paper
                                                     scissors

STEPS:

1. Plan and design the board game.
   a. Think of as many questions as possible about the topic you have studied (at least 30--the more the better!).
   b. Make a rough sketch of how you want the board to look (see examples).
   c. Make a set of rules for the game. Keep them simple!

2. Construct the game.
   a. Copy the questions on the index cards. Write a question and answer on one side of the card.
   b. Make a few "risk" cards that give directions: "Move ahead 3 spaces;" "Lose a turn;" "Take 2 turns;" "Go back to start;" "Exchange places with someone."

More steps are on the back...

© Johnsen and Johnson, 1986

GAME   76b

   c. Either draw squares or circles on the poster board for the spaces for the markers to move, or cut out squares or circles from construction paper and glue them to the board.
   d. Decorate the board with pictures or designs to make it appealing.
   e. Collect markers for the players to use, or make them out of colored paper.
   f. Write the rules neatly on construction paper and glue them to the back of the game.
      Consider a variation of some of the following rules:
      1) The object of the game is to get to the finish before anyone else.
      2) Place all players' markers at the start position.
      3) Roll the die to see who goes first (highest number) and continue in a clockwise rotation (the person to the left goes next).
      4) Each player rolls the die and moves the number of spaces indicated. Draw a card and try to answer the question. If correct, move ahead one space. If incorrect, move back a space.
      5) If you land on a space with someone else's marker, they must go back to start.
   g. Keep all markers, question cards and dice in the box.

3. Evaluate the game.
   a. When the game board is completed, play it with someone and see if it works. Ask the other player to help you improve it.
   b. Consider: Do you have enough questions? Were the questions too easy or too difficult? Did the game last too long or not long enough? Was is enjoyable?
   c. Make the necessary corrections.
   d. Explain the game to the class and invite everyone to play!

© Johnsen and Johnson, 1986

DEVELOP THE PRODUCT   RESOURCE CARD   77

GAME   EXAMPLES

© Johnsen and Johnson, 1986

DEVELOP THE PRODUCT   RESOURCE CARD   78

GRAPH

WHAT IS A GRAPH?

A graph is a diagram that shows the relationship between sets of numbers and some other factor. It shows comparisons clearly with a small amount of data.

There are four kinds of graphs discussed in the Resource Cards:

- line graph
- bar graph
- pictograph
- pie graph

© Johnsen and Johnson, 1986

DEVELOP THE PRODUCT   RESOURCE CARD   79

GRAPH   LINE GRAPH

HOW DO I MAKE A LINE GRAPH?

Materials: two sets of numbers   ruler
              graph paper   pencil

STEPS:

1. Plan the information that will go on the graph.
   a. Look at the numbers you collected in the study.
   b. Decide which information will be placed on the horizontal line and which will go on the vertical line. (Note: In most studies the time data, *i.e.*, days, months, years, go on the horizontal line.)
   c. Decide how many squares on the graph paper will be used for the horizontal and vertical lines of the graph. Try to balance the graph so that the horizontal and vertical lines are approximately the same length.

More steps are on the back...

© Johnsen and Johnson, 1986

79b

GRAPH   LINE GRAPH

STEPS (continued):

2. Draw the line graph.
   a. On the graph paper, draw the horizontal and vertical lines, long enough to accommodate the information you are showing.
   b. Plot the points on the graph where the horizontal and vertical lines cross (not in the spaces on the graph paper) by penciling a small dot for each piece of information.
   c. When all points are plotted, draw a line to connect all the points.
   d. It is possible for the line graph to have more than one line on the same graph. A second set of data can be plotted on the graph for comparison (see example).
   e. Label all parts of the graph--title of the graph, vertical axis, horizontal axis, line or lines drawn.

Examples of line graphs are on the next Resource Card...

© Johnsen and Johnson, 1986

HOW TO DEVELOP A GRAPH

RESOURCE CARDS 80-82

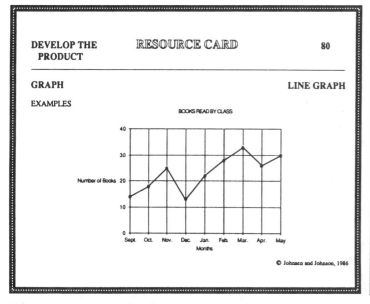

DEVELOP THE PRODUCT   RESOURCE CARD   80

GRAPH   LINE GRAPH

EXAMPLES

BOOKS READ BY CLASS

© Johnsen and Johnson, 1986

DEVELOP THE PRODUCT   RESOURCE CARD   82

GRAPH   PICTOGRAPH

HOW DO I MAKE A PICTOGRAPH?

Materials: two sets of numbers   paper
            ruler   pencil

STEPS:

1. Plan the graph.
   a. Pictographs are similar to line and bar graphs. However, pictures instead of lines and bars are used to impart information.
   b. Choose the pictures you will use to represent the data. Usually pictures are used that reflect the kind of information you are expressing. For example, if the graph is about money, "$'s" or pictures of coins might be used.
   c. Decide how many of how much each symbol will represent. For example, one coin might represent $100.00. If you wanted to show $300.00 on the graph, three coins would be used. If you wanted to show only $50.00, then a picture of a half coin would be used.

   More steps are on the back...

© Johnsen and Johnson, 1986

DEVELOP THE PRODUCT   RESOURCE CARD   81

GRAPH   BAR GRAPH

HOW DO I MAKE A BAR GRAPH?

Materials: two sets of numbers   ruler
            graph paper, 10 inches to an inch   pencil or colored pencils

STEPS:

1. Follow the steps presented under line graphs. Instead of placing dots and drawing lines, place a mark and color in the columns or "bars."

2. Bars can be draw vertically or horizontally.

   Examples are on the back...

© Johnsen and Johnson, 1986

82b

GRAPH   PICTOGRAPH

STEPS (continued):

2. Draw the pictograph.
   a. Because each symbol must be the same size, make one symbol and copy or trace it for all the other symbols. You may either cut them out and paste on the graph, or you may draw them directly on the graph.
   b. As you draw or paste on the symbols, keep them in a straight line or column.
   c. Label the graph, including a key that tells what the symbols represent.

BOOKS READ BY CLASS

Sept.
Oct.
Nov.
Dec.
Jan.
Feb.

= 5 books

© Johnsen & Johnson, 1986

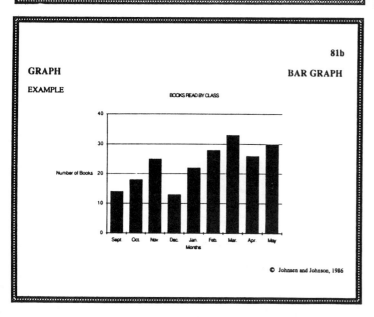

81b

GRAPH   BAR GRAPH

EXAMPLE

BOOKS READ BY CLASS

© Johnsen and Johnson, 1986

HOW TO DEVELOP A GRAPH AND A POSTER   RESOURCE CARDS 83-84

DEVELOP THE PRODUCT   RESOURCE CARD   83

GRAPH   PIE GRAPH

HOW DO I MAKE A PIE GRAPH?

Materials: several sets of numbers and data   paper, unlined
             protractor   ruler
             compass or round object   pencil

STEPS:

1. Plan the pie graph.
   a. Convert the numbers into percentages. Do this by dividing one part by the total number.
   b. Figure out how many degrees each number will represent, then multiply the percentage by 360 (the number of degrees in a circle).

2. Draw the pie graph.
   a. Use the compass (or a round object) and draw a circle the size you desire.
   b. Use the protractor to mark the number of degrees for each number on the graph.
   c. Use the ruler to divide the circle into parts and draw lines to the center of the circle.
   d. Label the parts of the graph so that the information is clear to the reader.

Examples are on the back...

© Johnsen and Johnson, 1986

DEVELOP THE PRODUCT   RESOURCE CARD   84

POSTER

HOW DO I MAKE A POSTER?

Materials: posterboard   ruler
             scratch paper   glue
             felt marker or crayons   pencil/eraser
                                          pictures, drawings, etc.

STEPS:

1. Plan the poster.
   a. The poster should have a border around the outside, a title in large, bold letters, pictures or drawings, and labels or short written descriptions.
   b. Decide how you want the poster to look and make a rough sketch on scratch paper. (Remember to keep it simple with only a few pictures, charts, and so on, and large letters to label.)
   c. On the posterboard, make a border around the outside using the ruler and pencil. Measure from the outer edge 1 - 2 inches and mark it in several places around the entire poster. With a pencil, join the marks using the ruler as a straight edge. Put all pictures and drawings inside the border.

More steps are on the back...

© Johnsen & Johnson, 1986

83b

GRAPH   PIE GRAPH

EXAMPLE

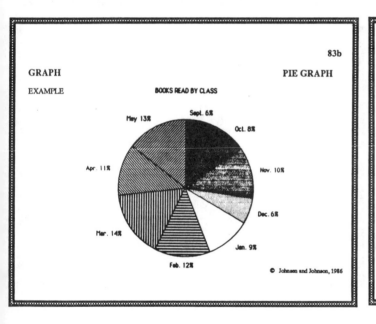

BOOKS READ BY CLASS

© Johnsen and Johnson, 1986

84b

POSTER

STEPS (Continued):

   d. Collect all the information you want to include on the poster and lay it loosely on the poster, arranging it evenly. Make sure that you include room to put labels and written descriptions.
   e. Decide how large the title letters should be and use the ruler and pencil to draw lightly straight lines as a guide. Make three lines to guide the top, middle, and bottom of the letter, such as:

   ```
   _____
   - - - - - - - - - - - - - - - - -
   _____
   ```

2. Create the poster.
   a. Draw the title letters in pencil or use large rub-on or stick-on letters.
   b. When they are spaced correctly, go over the penciled letters in ink.
   c. Glue the pictures or drawings to the poster board where you had them arranged.
   d. Add the labels or written descriptions.
   e. Either emphasize the border with an ink line or erase the pencil line.

border

© Johnsen and Johnson, 1986

HOW TO DEVELOP A PUPPET SHOW AND A REPORT

DEVELOP THE PRODUCT — RESOURCE CARD — 85

PUPPET SHOW

HOW DO I CREATE A PUPPET SHOW?

Materials: vary, depending on the kind of show
index cards

STEPS:

1. Plan the puppet show.
   a. Decide what topic, theme, or message you want to be the focus.
   b. Write the ideas you want to include on index cards.
   c. Sequence the cards. Order them by what you want to happen first, second, and so on.
   d. Decide how many characters will be in the play and who will play each part. You may want to include a narrator, someone who tells what is happening in the story.
   e. Using the note cards, write what each character will say.
   f. Decide how the play will be presented, what the stage will look like (behind a table covered with a sheet, or in a large cardboard box, such as a refrigerator box, with a hole cut out for the puppets), what props should be included in the set.
   g. Plan what kind of puppets to use (paper sack puppets, finger puppets, pencil puppets, papier maché puppets, rubber glove puppets). See examples on next card.

More steps are on the back...

© Johnsen and Johnson, 1986

DEVELOP THE PRODUCT — RESOURCE CARD — 87

REPORT — ORAL

HOW DO I PRESENT AN ORAL REPORT?

Materials: notes from topic studied   3" X 5" index cards
pencil

STEPS:

1. Plan the report.
   a. Find out how long you have to present your report.
   b. Decide what is the most important information you want your audience to learn.
   c. Write the main ideas of the report on index cards.
   d. Decide if you have other materials to show the class (posters, drawings, etc.).

2. Practice the presentation.
   a. Use the index cards and practice the report out loud until you are comfortable with it.
   b. Use a mirror, a tape recorder, or someone to listen to you.
   c. Time the presentation to make sure that it is within the given time limits.

© Johnsen & Johnson, 1986

85b

PUPPET SHOW

STEPS (continued):

2. Make the puppets and stage.

3. Present the production.
   a. Practice reading the script with the players before using the puppets.
   b. Make sure that all players speak loudly and keep their faces turned toward the audience (even though they are out of sight).
   c. Put the puppets in order of how they will appear in the show.
   d. Practice reading the script using the puppets.
   e. Time the show to see approximately how long it lasts.
   f. Plan a time with the teacher to present the show to the class.

Examples are on next Resource Card...

© Johnsen and Johnson, 1986

DEVELOP THE PRODUCT — RESOURCE CARD — 88

REPORT — WRITTEN

HOW DO I WRITE A REPORT?

Materials: paper   notes from topic studied
pencil   pen, typewriter or word processor

STEPS:

1. Plan and organize the report.
   a. Look over the notes or outline you made when you were researching the topic.
   b. Think about what you want to tell the audience. You may include:
      1) a statement of the question you are researching (what exactly did you study)
      2) discussion of the question (why you decided to study the question)
      3) the method (how you studied the question)
      4) the results (what did you find out in your study)
      5) conclusions (what answers did you find to the question)
      6) bibliography (what resources, books, magazines, materials did you use)
      7) acknowledgements (thanks to the people who helped you)
   c. Write a rough draft, skipping every other line to leave room for corrections. It is not uncommon for great thinkers to write at least three rough drafts.

More steps are on the back...

© Johnsen & Johnson, 1986

DEVELOP THE PRODUCT — RESOURCE CARD — 86

PUPPET SHOW — EXAMPLES

Paper Sack Puppet

Rubber Glove Puppet

Spoon Puppet

© Johnsen and Johnson, 1986

REPORT - WRITTEN   **88b**

STEPS (continued):

   d. Try to write the report using your own words. If you must use someone else's words, remember to use quotation marks and give credit to the source.
   e. Decide if you want to include pictures, drawings, graphs, charts in the paper.
   f. Give the report a title.

2. Write the report.
   a. Read over the rough draft.
      1) Does it flow nicely from one idea to the next (transition)?
      2) Does is say what you want it to say?
      3) Does it sound like your work and not a rewriting of a book?
   b. Make the necessary additions and corrections in pencil.
   c. In pen and on good paper, write the report in your best handwriting, type it, or have someone else type it.
   d. Include a title page. If your teacher does not give you specific guidelines, include
      1) Title of the report   4) Teacher's name
      2) Date report is due   5) Subject
      3) Your name

3. Proofread the report.
   a. Does the report look neat?
   b. Are all the words spelled correctly.
      1) You may have someone else proofread for spelling.
      2) Use white-out to correct spelling mistakes.
   c. Is is punctuated correctly?

© Johnsen & Johnson, 1986

HOW TO DEVELOP A TAPE RECORDING AND A TELEVISION SHOW

DEVELOP THE PRODUCT   RESOURCE CARD   89

TAPE RECORDING

HOW DO I MAKE A TAPE RECORDING?

Materials: tape recorder
              blank cassette tape
              written script

STEPS:

1. Plan the script.
   a. Decide what you want to tell the audience.
   b. Write a script to guide you. Include exactly what you will say and what others will say, if you are including anyone else.
   c. If you are recording an interview, you may write a list of possible questions you will ask the person. Tell them before the interview the kinds of questions you will ask, so that they can prepare some answers, if they wish.
   d. Practice what you will say before you turn on the tape recorder.

More steps are on the back...

© Johnson and Johnson, 1986

DEVELOP THE PRODUCT   RESOURCE CARD   90

TELEVISION SHOW

HOW DO I MAKE A TELEVISION SHOW?

Materials: shoe box   two pencils
              roll of paper   pencil
              pictures   crayons or felt markers
                                tape

STEPS:

1. Plan the television show.
   a. Plan what you want the television show to say.
   b. Decide what pictures you need.
   c. Either draw and color the pictures or cut them from magazines. Make sure that your pictures are smaller than the end of the box.
   d. Write what you will say for each picture.
   e. Don't forget to include a title page!

More steps are on the back...

© Johnson and Johnson, 1986

89b

TAPE RECORDING

STEPS (continued):

2. Make the recording.
   a. Try to record in a quiet area.
   b. Keep the microphone steady and approximately 10 - 15 inches away from your mouth.
   c. Watch the recording indicator to make sure that the sound level is correct. If the recorder does not have an indicator, check it by saying a few words into the recorder, wind it back, then listen to the sound. Make necessary adjustments.
   d. Give the title of the what you are presenting, such as, "This is an interview with Dr. Young about color photography."
   e. Speak clearly and slowly, but naturally.
   f. You may use soft music for the background, or at the beginning or ending of the tape.
   g. If you want someone to do something, give them exactly short, clear instructions, such as, "Turn to page 63 and read the first paragraph."
   h. When the tape is finished, tell the listener to turn off the recorder and rewind the tape.

3. Evaluate the recording.
   a. Have someone else listen to the tape to see if the information is clear and understandable.
   b. Make the necessary changes.

© Johnson & Johnson, 1986

90b

TELEVISION SHOW

STEPS (continued):

2. Make the set.
   a. Gather materials needed--box, 2 pencils, pictures, tape and a roll of paper (or several sheets taped together).
   b. Cut end out of the box.
   c. Cut the roll of paper slightly smaller than the end of the box.
   d. Paste the pictures onto the roll of paper in the correct order from left to right.
   e. Punch two holes the size of the pencils in the top of the box near the cut-out end of box.
   f. Insert the pencils and tape ends of the roll of paper to each pencil. Roll the paper around the pencils, then roll all the paper onto the right pencil.
   g. Roll the left pencil to begin the show.

3. Produce the show.
   a. Set a time for the class to watch the show.
   b. Place set in a central spot in the room, slightly higher than student's heads, so they can all see.
   c. As you roll the pictures, speak clearly to the viewers.

© Johnson and Johnson, 1986

HOW TO DEVELOP A TIME LINE

RESOURCE CARDS 91-92

DEVELOP THE PRODUCT   RESOURCE CARD   91

TIME LINE

WHAT IS A TIME LINE?

    A time line is a graphic way to show a sequence of events.

HOW DO I DEVELOP A TIME LINE?

Materials: posterboard or paper   pencil
               ruler   felt marker or crayons
                                           pictures or drawings

STEPS:

1. Plan the time line.
   a. Determine which years will be included in the time line.
   b. Decide whether the time line will run horizontally or vertically.
   c. Determine whether you will use pictures, drawings, special lettering or any graphic design on the time line.

More steps are on the back...

© Johnsen and Johnson, 1986

DEVELOP THE PRODUCT   RESOURCE CARD   92

TIME LINE

EXAMPLE OF A TIME LINE:

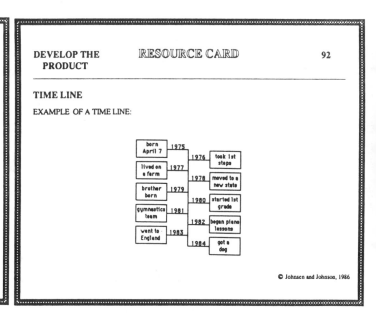

© Johnsen and Johnson, 1986

                                                91b

TIME LINE

STEPS (continued):

   d. Decide how long the line will be (are you using poster board, notebook paper, computer paper, etc?).
   e. Figure out how long each time period will be. For example, one-half inch could equal one year, five years, one hundred years or any time period you choose.

2. Draw the time line.
   a. Use a ruler and pencil to draw the time line.
   b. Divide the time line into specific time periods.
   c. In pencil, write the dates and information beside the time line.
   d. Place the pictures or drawings on the paper. When you are satisfied with the way they are arranged, glue them to the paper.
   e. Write a title for the time line. Use a pencil and ruler to center the letters evenly.
   f. Go over all the penciled letters in ink. Erase all pencil lines gently.

© Johnsen and Johnson, 1986

LESSON 25: OVERVIEW

Concepts: 1. Oral report
                 2. Display

Objective: The students will be able to present their products orally or in a display.

Materials: 1. Resource Cards 93, 94, 95, 96
                 2. Student Booklet, page 21
                 3. Blank overhead or chalkboard

Evaluation: Were the students able to present their products orally or in a display using the described steps?

Procedure:

1. Discuss with the students the importance of presenting the product. Have them identify reasons. Some of the reasons might include the following (**see Resource Card 93**):

   • Others can learn from your information.
   • You can get ideas from others.
   • You can improve the product.
   • Others can help evaluate the product.
   • You can gain the support of others.

NOTE: Some products such as puppet or T.V. shows are presentations in and of themselves that will need to be practiced; however, students may decide to add a display and/or an oral report to show the steps that were involved in developing these final products.

2. Talk about the major ways of presenting a product to an audience: a display or an oral report. Tell them that in a display their presentation explains their products with or without their presence. Show them some display examples (**see Resource Card 96**). On the other hand, in an oral report they present their products themselves. Tell them that often both approaches are combined.

3. Have the students think of the selected audience. With the students, list on the board the advantages and disadvantages of each approach with this audience.

4. Decide what approach(es) would be best for the audience.

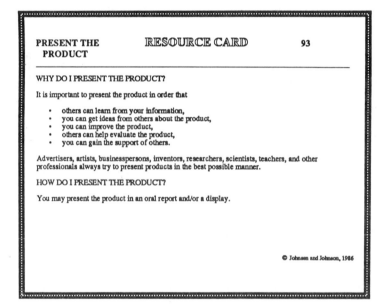

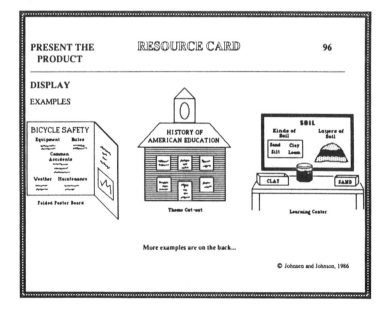

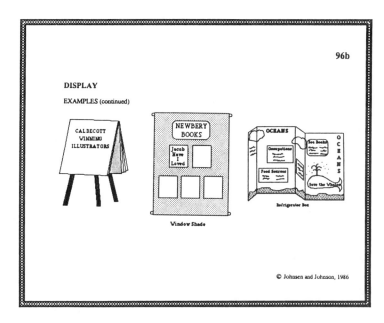

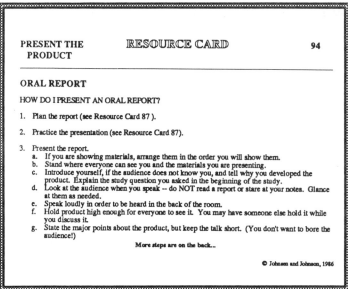

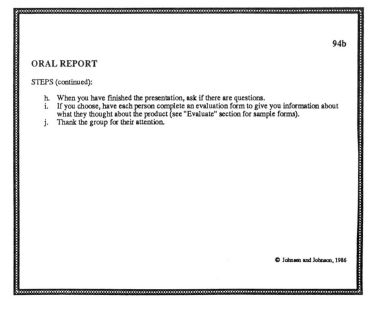

Procedure:

5. After selecting the approach, list the steps for the one selected on the chalkboard (see **Resource Cards 94 and 95**).

A. Steps for an oral report

- Plan the report.
- Practice the report.
- Arrange materials in order.
- Make sure everyone can see you.
- Introduce yourself.
- Look at the audience.
- Speak loud enough to be heard.
- Hold product so that it can be seen.
- State major points about product.
- Keep talk short.
- At end, ask for questions.
- Have persons complete evaluation.
- Thank the group.

B. Steps for a display

- Plan the display: find available space; visualize how display will look; secure needed materials; identify information to include in the display; estimate the time for setting up and the time for taking down.
- Make the display attractive: use colorful, eye-catching letters and materials; have products which explain study.
- Present the display: make notes if discussing display; invite audience to look at display closely; ask for questions.

6. Model a correct way of presenting the product through a display or by giving an oral report. Then model the incorrect way of presenting the product. Have the students point out the steps that were omitted.

Procedure:

7. If the students have planned to give oral reports, have them open the **Student Booklets** to **page 21**. Review the steps in the checklist.

8. Set a time for the students' practice presentations. Have the students work on their presentations.

9. On the day of their practice presentations, have the students use the questions in the **Student Booklets, page 21,** to evaluate one another.

10. After each presentation, have the students discuss the positive aspects first and then improvements that could be made before the final audience presentation. (You may wish to have another practice before the final presentation.)

11. After the final audience presentation, have the students discuss each other's improvements.

| PRESENT THE PRODUCT | RESOURCE CARD | 95 |

DISPLAY

HOW DO I PRESENT A DISPLAY?

1. Plan the display.
   a. Determine how much space is available for the display.
   b. Decide what the display should look like (see examples).
   c. Gather all materials necessary to make the display.
   d. Write a few notes on index cards to remind yourself of points you want to include in the presentation.

2. Make the display.
   a. Use colorful, cut-out letters for the title of the display, if possible. (Your teacher may have some stencils.)
   b. Include drawings, diagrams, pictures, and other items that will help to explain the study.

3. Present the display.
   a. Use the notes to discuss the display in an orderly manner.
   b. Invite the audience to look closely at the display after the presentation.
   c. Ask for and questions from the audience about the display.

Examples of displays are on the next card...

| PRESENT THE PRODUCT | SB 21 |

HOW DO I PRESENT THE PRODUCT?

PRESENTATION CHECKLIST

	YES	NO
1. Have I prepared the materials (handouts, overhead transparencies, display, etc.) needed in my presentation?	——	——
2. Have I practiced my presentation out loud (in front of a mirror or in front of another person)?	——	——
3. Have I timed my talk?	——	——
4. Have I made bried notes on index cards of the main ideas I will discuss?	——	——
5. When I practiced my presentation, did I:		
a. speak loud enough for the audience to hear?	——	——
b. tell the topic and study question?	——	——
c. glance at my notes only when I needed them?	——	——
d. show the display or materials smoothly along with my talk?	——	——
e. ask if there are any questions?	——	——
f. thank the audience for listening?	——	——

the final performance
which may take a minute
has been preceded by
many hours of rehearsal
L.R. Smith

LESSON 26: EVALUATION

Concepts: Evaluation

Objective: Students will select or design an evaluation form and evaluate their independent studies.

Materials: 1. Student Booklet, pages 22, 23, 24
                  2. Resource Card 97
                  3. Blank overhead or chalkboard

Evaluation: Did each student complete evaluation forms in analyzing strengths and weaknesses of his/her study?

Procedure:

NOTE: Students should know how they are going to be evaluated before they begin their independent studies in order for them to observe and improve the process of their studies.

1. Define *evaluation*. Use a definition from the students or the one on **Resource Card 97**: "Evaluation is examining the work that has been done on the independent study and analyzing the positive and negative points of the study."

2. Brainstorm with the students why it is important for them to evaluate their independent studies. (**Emphasize the need for improvement rather than grades.**)

3. List these reasons on the chalkboard or overhead. Star the reasons that the students feel are most important.

4. Look at the evaluation forms in the **Student Booklets, pages 22, 23, and 24.** Discuss with the students each evaluation form and explain each item of evaluation (*i.e*, what it means "to use time efficiently"). Have the students give both positive and negative examples for each criterion.

5. Decide which forms cover the reasons that the students felt were most important in Step 3. If they do, they might choose to use the forms in the Student Booklets. If not, they may decide to design their own forms.

6. Have the students each complete an evaluation form on himself/herself.

EVALUATE   RESOURCE CARD   97
THE STUDY

WHAT IS EVALUATION?

Evaluation is examining the work that has been done on the independent study and analyzing the positive and negative points of the study.

WHY SHOULD I EVALUATE THE STUDY?

Studies are evaluated in order to make improvements on this study and on future studies. It is helpful to have someone assist you in seeing what was good about the study and what improvements could be made.

WHO SHOULD EVALUATE THE STUDY?

You and the teacher may decide who will evaluate. Consider self, teacher, family members, experts, and audience.

© Johnsen and Johnson, 1986

EVALUATE THE STUDY   SB 22

SELF EVALUATION

Name _____ Date _____

Topic _____

Directions: Circle the number that best reflects your feelings about each statement.

	DISAGREE				AGREE
I had a well planned independent study.	1	2	3	4	5
I used my time efficiently.	1	2	3	4	5
I wrote a probing study question.	1	2	3	4	5
I used varied resources.	1	2	3	4	5
My research was extensive.	1	2	3	4	5
I developed a fine product.	1	2	3	4	5
My class presentation was effective.	1	2	3	4	5
I have good feelings about the independent study.	1	2	3	4	5

What I did well: _____

_____

The most difficult part was: _____

_____

What I would change: _____

_____

take a second look···

it costs you nothing.

Chinese Proverb

© Johnsen and Johnson, 1986

Procedure:

7. After the students have presented their final products of the study and have evaluated themselves, meet with each student individually to compare your evaluation with his/her evaluation.

8. When comparing and talking about the evaluations, remember these important points:

   • Focus on what the student has learned.

   • Focus on the process rather than the product.

   • Look for areas to improve in the next independent study.

   • Look for new questions (*i.e.*, new areas for study) that may have arisen in working on this independent study.

   • Be positive about each student's efforts.

one man's word
is no man's word;
we should quietly
hear both sides.
~goethe

EVALUATE THE STUDY   SB 23

TEACHER'S EVALUATION

Name _____ Date _____

Topic _____

Directions: Circle the number that best reflects your feelings about each statement.

	DISAGREE				AGREE
Student had a well planned independent study.	1	2	3	4	5
Student used time efficiently.	1	2	3	4	5
Student wrote a probing study question.	1	2	3	4	5
Student used varied resources.	1	2	3	4	5
Student's research was extensive.	1	2	3	4	5
Student developed a fine product.	1	2	3	4	5
Student's class presentation was effective.	1	2	3	4	5
I have good feelings about the student's independent study.	1	2	3	4	5

What was done well: _____

_____

_____

_____

Areas that need improving: _____

_____

_____

_____

© Johnsen and Johnson, 1986

EVALUATE THE STUDY   SB 24

EVALUATE ME!
(Evaluation by Audience)

Presenter(s) _____ Date _____

Topic _____

Directions: Check (√) the line that best describes how you feel about each phrase.

The presenter:

	YES	NOT SURE	NO
spoke clearly	—	—	—
looked at the audience	—	—	—
told the study question	—	—	—
answered the study question	—	—	—
made the information understandable	—	—	—
used a visual aid	—	—	—

I learned _____

_____

The most interesting part of the presentation was: _____

_____

Why? _____

_____

In the lesson I:

___ listened   ___ asked questions
___ discussed   ___ answered question
___ read something   ___ made something
___ other _____

Questions I have about the study: _____

_____

_____

© Johnsen and Johnson, 1986

APPENDIX A

SELECTED REFERENCES

SELECTED REFERENCES

Alexander, W., & Hines, V. *Independent study in the secondary schools.* New York: Holt, 1967.

Atwood, B.S. *Building independent learning skills.* Palo Alto, CA: Learning Handbooks, 1974.

Beggs, D., & Buffie, E. *Independent study: Bold new venture.* Bloomington: Indiana University Press, 1965.

Brady, J. *The craft of interviewing.* New York, NY: Vintage, 1976.

Burns, M. *The book of think.* Boston, MA: Little, Brown, 1976.

Draze, D., & Wood-Schnare. *Asking questions, finding answers.* San Luis Obsipo, CA: Dandy Lion, 1979.

Dressel, P., & Thompson, M.M. *Independent study.* San Francisco, CA: Jossey Bass, 1973.

Cline, S. *A practical guide to independent study.* New York, NY: Trillium Press, 1980.

Eberle, R.F. *Scamper.* Buffalo, NY: D.O.K., 1971.

Eberle, R.F. *Scamper on .* Buffalo, NY: D.O.K.

Eberle, R.F., & Stanish, B. *CPS for kids.* Buffalo, NY: D.O.K., 1980.

Forgan, H. *Read all about it!* Santa Monica, CA: Goodyear Publishing, 1979.

Forte, I., & MacKenzie, J. *The teacher's planning pak and guide to individualized instruction.* Nashville, Tenn.: Incentive Publications, 1978.

Heuer, J., Koprowicz, A., & Harris, R. *M.A.G.I.C. Kits.* Mansfield Center, Conn.: Creative Learning Press, 1980.

Homeratha, L., & Treffinger, D. *Independent study folders.* Buffalo, NY: D.O.K., 1980.

It takes teaching: a systematic approach to independent study. Dallas, TX: Dallas Independent School District, 1980.

Issac, S., & Michael, W. *Handbook in research and evaluation.* San Diego, CA: EdITS Pub., 1980.

Johnson, D.W., & Johnson, R.T. Learning together and alone. Englewood Cliffs, NJ: Prentice-Hall, 1975.

Kaplan, S., Kaplan, J., Madsen, S., & Gould, B. *Change for children* (revised edition). Santa Monica, CA: Goodyear, 1980.

Kaplan, S., Madsen, S., & Gould, B. *The big book of independent study.* Santa Monica, CA: Goodyear, 1976.

Karnes, F., & Collins, E. *Handbook of instructional resources and references for teaching the gifted.* Boston: Allyn and Bacon, 1984.

Knowles, M. *Self-directed learning.* Chicago, IL: Follett, 1975.

Mathers, F.M. *Entomology: investigative activities for could-be bug buffs.* Mansfield Center, CT: Creative Learning Press, 1978.

Simons, R. *Recyclopedia.* Boston: Houghton Mifflin, 1976.

Stewart, E.D., & Dean, M.J. *The almost whole earth catalog of process oriented enrichment materials.* Mansfield Center, CT: Creative Learning Press, 1980.

The I in independent study. Dallas, TX: Dallas Independent School District, 1980.

Treffinger, D.J. *Encouraging creative learning for the gifted and talented: A handbook of methods and techniques.* Ventura, CA: Ventura County Supt. of Schools, 1980.

Treffinger, D., Nash, D., & Homeratha, L. *Independent study folders--Secondary.* Buffalo, NY: D.O.K., 1981.

Up Periscope! Dallas, Texas: Dallas Independent School District, 1977.

Vezza, T., & Bagley, M. *The investigation of real problems.* Woodcliff Lake, NJ: Educational Institutes and Consulting Associates, 1979.

Weber, P. *Question quest.* Buffalo, NY: D.O.K., 1978.

Webster, D. *How to do a science project.* New York, NY: Franklin Watts, 1974.

Wurman, R.S. (Ed.). *Yellow pages of learning resources.* Cambridge, MA: MIT Press, 1972.

Zarchy, H. *Let's make more things.* New York, NY: Alfred Knopf, 1943.

Zarchy, H. *Let's make something.* New York, NY: Alfred Knopf, 1941.

APPENDIX B

RESOURCES

EVALUATION CHART

CRITERIA

C. _____

B. _____

A. _____

T O T A L

	A	B	C	
1.				
2.				
3.				
4.				
5.				

adapted from Texas Future Problem Solving

WHICH TYPE OF THINKING?

_____ How are daisies and bluebonnets alike? how are they different?

_____ How might you define the word "hero?"

_____ How might you plan a family reunion?

_____ Who were the first five presidents of the United States?

_____ Who do you think is the best writer in class? Why?

_____ What improvements could you make to the computer?

_____ What are the pro's and con's of rock music?

_____ How might you make a model to demonstrate your idea?

_____ Do you like living in this city? Why or why not?

YACHTS

I. **History**

  A. **Early commercial uses**

   1. **Revenue marine**
   2. **Privateers**
   3. **Slavery**

  B. **Early sporting uses**

   1. **World's Fair of 1851**
   2. **New York Yacht Club**

II. **Current yachts**

  A. **Daysailers**

   1. **Characteristics**
   2. **Use**

  B. **Offshore ocean racers**

   1. **Characteristics**
   2. **Use**

III. **Races**

  A. **"One-design" race**

   1. **Boat specifications**
   2. **Location**

  B. **"Handicap" race**

   1. **Handicap specifications**
   2. **Location**

WORDS:

.

OUTLINES:

TITLE A:

I.

    A.
    B.

II.

    A.
    B.
    C.
    D.
    E.
    F.
    G.
    H.
    I.

TITLE B:

I.

    A.
    B.

II.

    A.
    B.

III.

    A.
    B.

IV.

    A.
    B.

TITLE A:
I.
   A.
      1.
      2.
   B.
      1.
      2.
      3.
II.
   A.
      1.
      2.
      3.
   B.
      1.
      2.
      3.
   C.
      1.
      2.
      3.
   D.
      1.
      2.
      3.
   E.
      1.
      2.
      3.
   F.
      1.
      2.
      3.
   G.
      1.
      2.
      3.
   H.
      1.
      2.
      3.
   I.
      1.
      2.
      3.

TITLE B:
I.
   A.
      1.
      2.
   B.
      1.
      2.
II.
   A.
      1.
      2.
   B.
      1.
      2.
III.
   A
      1.
      2.
   B.
      1.
      2.
IV.
   A.
      1.
      2.
   B.
      1.
      2.

James DeMesquita
Glendale Elementary
24 Congress Avenue
Glendale, OH 45246

October 31, 1986

Ms. Molly Lee
Green Thumb Nursery
15 Maple Circle
Cincinnati, OH 45246

Dear Ms. Lee:

I am working on an independent study project about plants in my fourth grade class. I would like to visit your nursery and learn about the plants that are natural to Ohio. Please let me know if there might be a time that would be convenient to come visit.

I look forward to hearing from you.

Sincerely,

James DeMesquita

P.S. I am particularly interested in wildflowers.

cc. Mr. Masters, Teacher
Mrs. Sussman, Principal

QUESTIONNAIRE

_____

#_____

Fill in the information below:

1. _____Boy _____Girl

2. _____ Birthday

3. _____Grade

_____

Check only one line which is nearest to the amount of time you spend each evening watching television and doing homework:

4. The approximate amount of time I study each night:

    ___ less than 30 minutes
    ___30 minutes to one hour
    ___more than one hour
    ___more than two hours
    ___more than three hours

5. The approximate amount of time I watch T.V. each night:

    ___less than 30 minutes
    ___30 minutes to one hour
    ___more than one hour
    ___more than two hours
    ___more than three hours
    ___I don't have a T.V.

_____

Now complete each statement below with **one** answer:

6. My favorite subject in school is _____.

7. My favorite T. V. show is _____.

OBSERVATION FORM

DAYS OF WEEK					
TIME	M	T	W	T	F
4:00					
4:30					
5:00					
5:30					
6:00					
6:30					
7:00					
7:30					
8:00					
8:30					
9:00					
9:30					
10:00					
10:30					
11:00					

CODE: Watching T.V. =   Subject or title of T.V.
Studying =   show is written in the
Other activity =   box next to time and day

116   © Johnsen and Johnson, 1986

INDEPENDENT STUDY SKILL SEQUENCE

INTRODUCTION

1. Can name and describe the steps of independent study
2. Can tell what a topic is

SELECT A TOPIC

1. Can brainstorm topics
2. Can gather information about topic
3. Can select one topic using an evaluation procedure
   a. Can identify criteria for selecting a topic
   b. Can rate topics according to criteria

ORGANIZE A TOPIC

1. Can organize a topic using descriptions
   a.. Can brainstorm characteristics
   b. Can use a network in describing a topic
2. Can organize a topic using comparisons
   a. Can brainstorm comparisons
   b. Can use a chart in comparing topics
3. Can organize a topic using causes and effects
   a. Can brainstorm changes, causes, and/or effects
   b. Can use a chart in examining changes, causes, effects
4. Can organize a topic using problems and solutions
   a. Can brainstorm problems and/or solutions
   b. Can use SCAMPER techniques for problems, solutions

ASK QUESTIONS

1. Can identify good study questions
2. Can write good study questions using "W" words
3. Can write questions requiring little thinking
4. Can write questions requiring more thinking
5. Can write questions requiring most thinking
6. Can select questions using an evaluation procedure
   a. Can identify criteria for selecting questions
   b. Can rate questions according to criteria
7. Can organize questions into a sequence for study
   a. Can develop a sequence with questions
   b. Can place these questions into outline form

USE A STUDY METHOD

1. Can describe topic with numbers or facts
2. Can examine past or history of a topic
3. Can look at development of topic
4. Can observe a person, a group or something closely
5. Can compare one thing with another using numbers
6. Can examine an improvement made to a problem
7. Can conduct experimental research
8. Can collect factual information
9. Can select a nonbiased sample
10. Can examine reliability of research instrument
11. Can examine validity of research instrument
12. Can make valid generalizations about study
13. Can describe topic using the average, mode and range
14. Can examine relationships using correlations

COLLECT INFORMATION

1. Can brainstorm
   a. Can use SCAMPER skills
   b. Can evalute brainstorm list
2. Can classify
3. Can interview
4. Can summarize
   a. Can make generalizations
   b. Can describe the parts
   c. Can identify causes and effects
   d. Can make comparisons
   e. Can show a sequence
   f. Can identify problems and solutions
5. Can conduct a survey
   a. Can conduct a face-to-face interview
   b. Can conduct a telephone interview
   c. Can develop a questionnaire
   d. Can analyze results
6. Can take notes
7. Can outline
   a. Can outline main ideas
   b. Can outline subtopics
   c. Can outline details
8. Can write a business letter

DEVELOP A PRODUCT

1. Can brainstorm products
2. Can select a product
   a. Can identify criteria for selecting a product
   b. Can rate products according to criteria
3. Can plan the development of product
4. Can develop a product
   a. Book
   b. Diagram
   c. Diorama
   d. Filmstrip
   e. Game
   f. Graph
   g. Poster
   h. Puppet Show
   i. Report
   j. Tape Recording
   k. Television Show
   l. Time line
   m. Other_____

PRESENT THE PRODUCT

1. Can present the product orally
2. Can use a display
3. Other_____

EVALUATE THE STUDY

1. Can do a self evaluation
2. Can compare own evaluation

INDEPENDENT STUDY SKILL CORRELATION CHART

AREA OF INDEPENDENT STUDY	TEACHER GUIDE	STUDENT BOOKLET	RESOURCE CARDS	OVER HEAD	HAND OUT	OTHER
INTRODUCTION						
1. Can name and describe the steps of independent study	1-3	1-3	1			
2. Can tell what a topic is	1	2, 4	1-3			
SELECT A TOPIC						
1. Can brainstorm topics	4, 48-50		34			
2. Can gather information about topic	7-8, 46-76	2, 15	34-62			
3. Can select one topic using an evaluation procedure	5-6	2, 5-6	4	1		
a. Can identify criteria for selecting a topic	5	5-6	4	1		
b. Can rate topics according to criteria	5-6	6		1		
ORGANIZE A TOPIC						
1. Can organize a topic using descriptions	9-10, 57-59	2, 7	5, 44			
a. Can brainstorm characteristics	10, 48-50		34, 5			
b. Can use a network in describing a topic	10		5			
2. Can organize a topic using comparisons	11-12, 57-59	2, 7	6, 46			
a. Can brainstorm comparisons	11-12, 48-50		34, 6			
b. Can use a chart in comparing topics	11-12		6			
3. Can organize a topic using causes and effects	13-14, 57-59	2, 7	7, 45			
a. Can brainstorm changes, causes, effects	13-14, 48-50		34, 7			
b. Can use chart examining changes, causes, effects	13-14		7			

INDEPENDENT STUDY SKILL CORRELATION CHART (CONTINUED)

AREA OF INDEPENDENT STUDY	TEACHER GUIDE	STUDENT BOOKLET	RESOURCE CARDS	OVER HEAD	HAND OUT	OTHER
ORGANIZE A TOPIC (CONTINUED)						
4. Can organize a topic using problems and solutions	15-16, 57-59	2, 7	8-9, 48			
a. Can brainstorm problems and/or solutions	15-16, 48-50		8, 34			
b. Can use SCAMPER techniques--problems, solutions	16, 49-50		35			
ASK QUESTIONS						
1. Can identify good study questions	17	2, 8	10			
2. Can write good study questions using "W" words	17-18	2	11			
3. Can write questions requiring little thinking	19	2, 9	12			
4. Can write questions requiring more thinking	20	2, 10	13			
5. Can write questions requiring most thinking	21	2, 11	14	2		
6. Can select questions using an evaluation procedure	23	2, 12-13		1		
a. Can identify criteria for selecting questions	17, 19-22	8, 12	10-14	1		
b. Can rate questions according to criteria	23	12-13		1		
7. Can organize questions into a sequence for study	24-25	2, 3	36, 60			
a. Can put questions in sequence	24-25, 51-52, 57-59		36, 47			
b. Can place these questions into outline form	24-25, 68-72	2, 3	60	3-5		
USE A STUDY METHOD						
1. Can describe topic with numbers or facts	26-27	2, 14	16-17			
2. Can examine past or history of a topic	26, 28	2, 14	18-19			

INDEPENDENT STUDY SKILL CORRELATION CHART (CONTINUED)

AREA OF INDEPENDENT STUDY	TEACHER GUIDE	STUDENT BOOKLET	RESOURCE CARDS	OVER HEAD	HAND OUT	OTHER
USE A STUDY METHOD (CONTINUED)						
3. Can look at development of topic	26, 29	2, 14	20-21			
4. Can observe a person, a group or something closely	26, 30	2, 14	22-23			
5. Can compare one thing with another using numbers	26, 31	2, 14	24-25			
6. Can examine an improvement made to a problem	26, 32	2, 14	26-27			
7. Can conduct experimental research	26, 33	2, 14	28-30			
8. Can collect factual information	26, 34	2, 14	31			
9. Can select a nonbiased sample	35-37		32		1	
10. Can examine reliability of research instrument	38-39, 40-45				1, 2	
11. Can examine validity of research instrument	39, 40-45				1, 2	
12. Can make valid generalizations about study	42-45, 57-59		43		1, 2	
13. Can describe topic using the average, mode and range	43-45				1, 2	
14. Can examine relationships using correlations	43-45		24-25		1, 2	
COLLECT INFORMATION						
1. Can brainstorm	46-47	2, 15	33			
a. Can use SCAMPER skills	48-50	2	34-35			
b. Can evalute brainstorm list	16, 49-50		35			
2. Can classify	51-52	2	36			
3. Can interview	53-56	2	37-40			

INDEPENDENT STUDY SKILL CORRELATION CHART (CONTINUED)

AREA OF INDEPENDENT STUDY	TEACHER GUIDE	STUDENT BOOKLET	RESOURCE CARDS	OVER HEAD	HAND OUT	OTHER
COLLECT INFORMATION						
4. Can summarize	40-45, 57-59	2	41-48			
a. Can make generalizations	42-43, 57-59			43		
b. Can describe the parts	9-10, 57-59		5, 44			
c. Can identify causes and effects	13-14, 57-59		7, 45			
d. Can make comparisons	11-12, 57-59		6, 46			
e. Can show a sequence	24-25, 51-52, 57-59		47			
f. Can identify problems and solutions	15-16, 57-59		8-9, 48			
5. Can conduct a survey	60-63	2	32, 49-53			
a. Can conduct a face-to-face interview	35-37, 60-63		32, 49, 51			
b. Can conduct a telephone interview	35-37, 60-63		32, 49, 51			
c. Can develop a questionnaire	35-37, 38-45, 60-63		32, 50			
d. Can analyze results	40-45, 63		53-55			
6. Can take notes	64-67	2	56-59			
7. Can outline	68-72	2	60	3-5		
a. Can outline main ideas	68-69		60	3-4		
b. Can outline subtopics	70		60	3-4		
c. Can outline details	71		60	3, 5		
8. Can write a business letter	73-76	2	61-62	6		

INDEPENDENT STUDY SKILL CORRELATION CHART (CONTINUED)

AREA OF INDEPENDENT STUDY	TEACHER GUIDE	STUDENT BOOKLET	RESOURCE CARDS	OVER HEAD	HAND OUT	OTHER
DEVELOP A PRODUCT						
1. Can brainstorm products	77-78	3, 16	63-65			
2. Can select a product	79, 81	3, 17-18	65-92			
a. Can identify criteria for selecting a product	79, 81	17-18				
b. Can rate products according to criteria	79, 81	17-18				
3. Can plan the development of product	80-81	19-20	65-92			
4. Can develop a product	82-90	3	65-92			
a. Book	82-83	3	66-69			
b. Diagram	83-84	3	70-73			
c. Diorama	84	3	74			
d. Filmstrip	84	3	75			
e. Game	85	3	76-77			
f. Graph	85-87	3	78-83			
g. Poster	87	3	84			
h. Puppet Show	88	3	85-86			
i. Report	88	3	87-88			
j. Tape Recording	89	3	89			
k. Television Show	89	3	90			
l. Time line	90	3	91-92			

INDEPENDENT STUDY SKILL CORRELATION CHART (CONTINUED)

AREA OF INDEPENDENT STUDY	TEACHER GUIDE	STUDENT BOOKLET	RESOURCE CARDS	OVER HEAD	HAND OUT	OTHER
PRESENT THE PRODUCT						
1. Can present the product orally	91-93	3, 21	93-94			
2. Can use a display	91-93	3	93, 95-96			
3. Other _____	91	3				
EVALUATE THE STUDY						
1. Can do a self evaluation	94-95	3, 22	97			
2. Can compare evaluations with others	94-95	3, 23-24	97			

125

INDEPENDENT STUDY AREA

SKILL

STUDENT NAME																				

NAME_____

■□□ Can do skill with teacher instruction
■■□ Can do skill without teacher instruction
■■■ Has done skill three times without teacher instruction

GRADE_____ **TEACHER**_____

INTRODUCTION

□□□ 1. Can name and describe the steps of independent study
□□□ 2. Can tell what a topic is

SELECT A TOPIC

□□□ 1. Can brainstorm topics
□□□ 2. Can gather information about topic
□□□ 3. Can select one topic using an evaluation procedure
□□□   a. Can identify criteria for selecting a topic
□□□   b. Can rate topics according to criteria

ORGANIZE A TOPIC

□□□ 1. Can organize a topic using descriptions
□□□   a.. Can brainstorm characteristics
□□□   b. Can use a network in describing a topic
□□□ 2. Can organize a topic using comparisons
□□□   a. Can brainstorm comparisons
□□□   b. Can use a chart in comparing topics
□□□ 3. Can organize a topic using causes and effects
□□□   a. Can brainstorm changes, causes, and/or effects
□□□   b. Can use a chart in examining changes, causes, effects
□□□ 4. Can organize a topic using problems and solutions
□□□   a. Can brainstorm problems and/or solutions
□□□   b. Can use SCAMPER techniques for problems, solutions

ASK QUESTIONS

□□□ 1. Can identify good study questions
□□□ 2. Can write good study questions using "W" words
□□□ 3. Can write questions requiring little thinking
□□□ 4. Can write questions requiring more thinking
□□□ 5. Can write questions requiring most thinking
□□□ 6. Can select questions using an evaluation procedure
□□□   a. Can identify criteria for selecting questions
□□□   b. Can rate questions according to criteria
□□□ 7. Can organize questions into a sequence for study
□□□   a. Can develop a sequence with questions
□□□   b. Can place these questions into outline form

USE A STUDY METHOD

□□□ 1. Can describe topic with numbers or facts
□□□ 2. Can examine past or history of a topic
□□□ 3. Can look at development of topic
□□□ 4. Can observe a person, a group or something closely
□□□ 5. Can compare one thing with another using numbers
□□□ 6. Can examine an improvement made to a problem
□□□ 7. Can conduct experimental research
□□□ 8. Can collect factual information
□□□ 9. Can select a nonbiased sample
□□□ 10. Can examine reliability of research instrument
□□□ 11. Can examine validity of research instrument
□□□ 12. Can make valid generalizations about study
□□□ 13. Can describe topic using the average, mode and range
□□□ 14. Can examine relationships using correlations

COLLECT INFORMATION

□□□ 1. Can brainstorm
□□□   a. Can use SCAMPER skills
□□□   b. Can evalute brainstorm list
□□□ 2. Can classify
□□□ 3. Can interview
□□□ 4. Can summarize
□□□   a. Can make generalizations
□□□   b. Can describe the parts
□□□   c. Can identify causes and effects
□□□   d. Can make comparisons
□□□   e. Can show a sequence
□□□   f. Can identify problems and solutions
□□□ 5. Can conduct a survey
□□□   a. Can conduct a face-to-face interview
□□□   b. Can conduct a telephone interview
□□□   c. Can develop a questionnaire
□□□   d. Can analyze results
□□□ 6. Can take notes
□□□ 7. Can outline
□□□   a. Can outline main ideas
□□□   b. Can outline subtopics
□□□   c. Can outline details
□□□ 8. Can write a business letter

DEVELOP A PRODUCT

□□□ 1. Can brainstorm products
□□□ 2. Can select a product
□□□   a. Can identify criteria for selecting a product
□□□   b. Can rate products according to criteria
□□□ 3. Can plan the development of product
□□□ 4. Can develop a product
□□□   a. Book
□□□   b. Diagram
□□□   c. Diorama
□□□   d. Filmstrip
□□□   e. Game
□□□   f. Graph
□□□   g. Poster
□□□   h. Puppet Show
□□□   i. Report
□□□   j. Tape Recording
□□□   k. Television Show
□□□   l. Time line
□□□   m. Other_____

PRESENT THE PRODUCT

□□□ 1. Can present the product orally
□□□ 2. Can use a display
□□□ 3. Other_____

EVALUATE THE STUDY

□□□ 1. Can do a self evaluation
□□□ 2. Can compare own evaluation

APPENDIX C

INDEX

Action research, 26, 32
Ask questions, 17-21, 23-25
    definition of good study question, 17
    by "W" words, 17-18
    evaluation of, 23
    little thinking, 19
    more thinking, 20
    most thinking, 21
    organize into sequence, 24-25
    outlining, 24-25
Audience, 94-95
    evaluation, 94-95

Book development, 82-83
Brainstorming, 4, 11-16, 48-50, 77-78
    causes and effects, 13-14
    comparisons, 11-12
    definition of, 4
    problems and solutions, 15-16
    products, 77-78
    SCAMPER techniques, 16, 49-50
    topics, 4
    ways of collecting information, 48-50

Case study research, 26, 30
Causes and effects, 13-14, 57-59
    brainstorming, 13-14
    definition of, 13
    organizing with, 13-14
    summarizing with, 57-59
Chart, 11-16
    of causes and effects, 13-14
    comparisons, 11-12
    problems and solutions, 15-16
Classify, 51-52
Collect information, 7-8, 40-76
    about topics, 7-8
    by brainstorming, 48-50
    by classifying, 51-52
    by interviewing, 7-8, 53-56
    by letter writing, 73-76
    by note taking, 64-67
    by outlining, 68-72
    by surveying, 60-63
    by summarizing, 40-45, 57-59
Comparisons, 11-12, 57-59
    brainstorming, 11-12
    definition of, 11
    organizing with, 11-12
    summarizing with, 57-59
Correlational research, 26, 31, 43-45
Criteria, 5, 17, 19-22, 79, 81
    for product selection, 79, 81
    for questions, 17, 19-22
    for topics, 5

Describing, 9-10, 26-27, 57-59
    in research, 26-27
    organizing with, 9-10
    parts, 9-10, 57-59
    summarizing with, 57-59
Develop a product, 77-90
    Book, 82-83
    Brainstorming products, 77-78
    Diagram, 83-84
    Diorama, 84
    Evaluating products, 79, 81
    Filmstrip, 84
    Game, 85
    Graph, 85-87
    Planning, 80-81
    Poster, 87
    Puppet show, 88
    Report, 88
    Tape recording, 89
    Television show, 89
    Time line, 90
Developmental research, 26, 29
Diagram development, 83-84
Diorama development, 84
Display, 91-93

Experimental research, 26, 33
Evaluating, 5-6, 23, 50, 79, 81, 94-95
    independent study, 94-95
    products, 79, 81
    questions, 23
    topics, 5-6
    ways of collecting information, 50

Filmstrip development, 84

Game development, 85
Generalization, 42-45, 57-59
Graph development, 85-87

Historical research, 26, 28

Independent study, 1-3
    definition of, 1
    steps of, 1-3
Interviewing, 7-8, 53-56
    face-to-face, 35-37, 60-63
    telephone, 35-37

Letter writing, 73-76
Little thinking, 19

More thinking, 20
Most thinking, 21

Network, 10
Nonbiased sample, 35-37
Note taking, 64-67

Oral presentation, 91-93
Organize a topic, 9-16
    definition of, 9
    by causes and effects, 13-14
    by comparisons, 11-12
    by descriptions, 9-10
    by problems and solutions, 15-16
Outlining, 24-25, 68-70
    details, 71
    questions, 24-25
    main ideas, 68-69
    subtopics, 70

Present the product, 91-93
    in a display, 91-93
    orally, 91-93
Poster development, 87
Problems and solutions, 15-16, 57-59
    organizing with, 15-16
    summarizing with, 57-59
Puppet show development, 88

Questionnaire, 35-36, 38-45, 60-63
    development of 35-36, 38-45, 60-63
Questions, 17-21, 24-25
    Good study, 17
    Little thinking, 19
    More thinking, 20
    Most thinking, 21
    Outlining, 24-25
    Sequencing, 24-25
    "W" words, 17-18

Report writing, 88
Reliability, 38-39, 40-45

Select a topic, 4-8
    brainstorm, 4
    evaluate, 5-6
    gather information, 7-8
Self evaluation, 94-95
Sequencing, 24-25, 57-59
    questions, 24-25
    to summarize, 57-59
SCAMPER, 16, 49-50
Study method, 26-45
    action, 26, 32
    case study, 26, 30
    correlation, 26, 31, 43-45
    descriptive, 26-27
    developmental, 26, 29
    experimental, 26, 33
    factual, 26, 34
    generalization in, 42-45, 57-59
    historical, 26, 28
    reliability of instrument, 38-39, 40-45
    summarizing results, 42-45

      use of nonbiased sample, 35-37
      validity of instrument, 39, 40-45
Summarizing, 40-45, 57-59
Surveying, 60-63

Tape recording, 89
Teacher evaluation, 94-95
Television show development, 89
Time line development, 90
Topic, 1, 4-8
      brainstorming, 4
      definition of, 1
      evaluating, 5-6
      gathering information about, 7-8

Validity, 39, 40-45

"W" words, 17-18